In the Kitchen with Mary & Martha

A **Cookbook** That Makes **Mealtime** a
Breeze for **Busy Women** Everywhere!

BARBOUR PUBLISHING

D0420114

(9) Stir
(10) Add l cp. flour, sugar, milk – Divide into
4 containers w/ l cp in
each – give to friends (3) to the
one left combine the following: 2/3 cp oil
3 eggs
½ tsp salt
1 tsp vanilla
1 – 1½ tsp. cinn.

Beat well w/ fork
Grease 2 loaf pans spr.
w/ sugar
Bake 325° 45 m
1 hr.
Cool 10 min – remove from pans
(Makes 2 loaves)
½ tsp. baking soda

Cover Art and interior illustrations by Margy Ronning
Cover and interior design by Greg Jackson/Jackson Design Co.

Published by Barbour Publishing, Inc., P.O. Box 719, Uhrichsville, Ohio 44683, www.barbourbooks.com

Our mission is to publish and distribute inspirational products offering exceptional value and biblical encouragement to the masses.

Member of the
Evangelical Christian
Publishers Association

Printed in China.
5 4 3 2 1

Dedication

To my husband, Kirk,
and my gifts from God, Keane and Kiley.
I love you.
Mary

To my mother, Wanda Royer, who never ceases to amaze
me with the way she gets a table full of dishes on by her
designated dinnertime—let alone one amazing dish.
Martha

A Special Greeting from Mary & Martha...

H i! Mary and Martha here. Thanks for joining us in the kitchen. We're so excited about our brand-new cookbook for you busybodies out there. Whether you're a busy mom to one or mom to a small army—or if you work hard all day and just don't want to think about spending your free time over a hot stove—you'll go plumb crazy over these one-dish wonders! Imagine...entire meals, snacks, and dinner additions you can cook up in one—yes, we said only one—dish!

One-Dish Wonders is chock-full of simple recipes for scrumptious snacks and meals your whole family will just plain love! And not only will these recipes make food preparation a snap, but cleanup will be, too. Just think of all you can do in your spare time: cuddle with the kiddos, take a trip to the day spa, curl up and read a good book, watch a favorite movie with the family...

In addition to equipping you with dozens of deliciously delightful, time-saving (and sanity-saving!) recipes, we'll be making appearances throughout this book with some down-home inspiration and helpful tips just for you. So be on the lookout, and...

Happy cooking!

MARY & MARTHA

The best things are the nearest: breath in your nostrils, light in your eyes,
flowers at your feet, duties at your hand, the path of Right just before you.
Do not grasp at the stars, but do life's plain common work as it comes,
certain that daily duties and daily bread are the sweetest things in life.

ROBERT LOUIS STEVENSON (1850–1894),
Scottish novelist, poet, and essayist

CONTENTS

"MOM, I'M HUNGRY!"
Simply Quick Snacks 9

OUT THE DOOR IN A FLASH
Meals on the Go 31

MIX IT ALL TOGETHER—& VOILÁ!
Casseroles & Other One-Dish Wonders 51

WHILE YOU WERE OUT. . .
Slow-Cooker Recipes 89

EASY, BREEZY ADDITIONS
Salads, Soups & Sides...115

FIVE & UNDER
5 Ingredients or Less 153

SIMPLY SWEET
Candies & Desserts 179

NIFTY SUBSTITUTIONS
A Little of This, Plus a Pinch of That................................. 209

WEIGHTS AND MEASURES KNOW-HOW
The Cheat Sheet 213

"MOM, I'M HUNGRY!"

Simply Quick Snacks

Make [food] simple and let things taste of what they are.

CURNONSKY (1872–1956), French writer

9/09 we found all kinds of snacks to put in this—each person can taylor make their own— :)

Munch Mix

1 (9 OUNCE) BAG SWEET AND SALTY SNACK MIX WITH CEREAL AND PRETZELS

1 (6 OUNCE) PACKAGE CORN SNACK (SUCH AS BUGLES)

1 (6 OUNCE) BOX CHEESE CRACKERS

1 CUP PEANUTS OR MIXED NUTS (OPTIONAL)

1 CUP CANDY-COATED CHOCOLATE PIECES (OPTIONAL)

Combine all ingredients in a large bowl. Serve.

Yield: 4 to 6 servings

* fried flavored goldfish
* shoestrings
* dryroasted honey peanuts

This snack mix is delightfully simple to prepare. Allow your kids to create a snack mix of their own—adding ingredients of their choice. They'll get a kick out of using their creative genius in the kitchen. And they just might surprise you with a tasty treat!

Sweet Snack Mix

1 CUP SALTED ROASTED PEANUTS

¼ CUP SEMISWEET CHOCOLATE CHIPS

1 TABLESPOON SUNFLOWER SEEDS

¼ CUP WHOLE ALMONDS

¼ CUP RAISINS

Combine all ingredients in a large bowl. Serve.

Yield: 4 to 6 servings

Ultimate Snack Mix

2 CUPS WHEAT SQUARES CEREAL
(SUCH AS WHOLE-GRAIN CHEX)

2 CUPS TOASTED OATS CEREAL

3 CUPS MINI PRETZEL STICKS

½ CUP SUNFLOWER SEEDS

½ CUP DRIED CRANBERRIES

1½ TABLESPOONS BUTTER

¼ CUP HONEY

2 TABLESPOONS VEGETABLE OIL

¼ CUP SUGAR

¾ TEASPOON GROUND CINNAMON

8 OUNCES MOZZARELLA CHEESE
CUBES

Toss the cereals, pretzel sticks, and sunflower seeds in a large mixing bowl;
set aside. Melt butter in a small saucepan. Stir in honey, vegetable oil, and
sugar. Bring to a boil, stirring occasionally. Remove from heat, then stir
in cinnamon and mix well. Pour over cereal mixture, stirring until evenly
coated. Spread cereal mixture in a baking pan and bake at 325° for 20
minutes (stirring after 10 minutes). Remove from oven and cool on waxed
paper. Add in dried cranberries and store in an airtight container until ready
to serve. Toss in cheese cubes just before serving.

Yield: 10 servings

Traditional Snack Mix

¼ CUP BUTTER OR MARGARINE

1¼ TEASPOONS SEASONED SALT

4½ TEASPOONS WORCESTERSHIRE SAUCE

2 CUPS CORN CEREAL

2 CUPS RICE CEREAL

2 CUPS WHEAT CEREAL

1 CUP SALTED MIXED NUTS

1 CUP MINI PRETZEL STICKS

In a large microwave-safe bowl, melt butter on HIGH for 30 seconds.
Stir in salt and sauce. Gradually add cereals, nuts, and pretzel sticks.
Microwave on HIGH for 5 to 6 minutes, stirring every 2 minutes. Spread
on waxed paper to cool.

Yield: 10 servings

*When measuring dry ingredients, especially if your
children are helping, chances are you'll wind up with
a mess on your countertop. Do your measuring over a
paper plate or a sheet of waxed paper. Spills can then
be picked up easily and returned to the canister.*

Trail Mix

½ CUP WALNUTS, COARSELY CHOPPED

½ CUP RAISINS

½ CUP DATES, CHOPPED

½ CUP DRIED APPLE SLICES, CHOPPED

½ CUP DRIED APRICOTS, CHOPPED

½ CUP SEMISWEET CHOCOLATE CHIPS

½ CUP ROUND OATS CEREAL (SUCH AS CHEERIOS)

Combine all ingredients in a large bowl. Store in an airtight container.
Yield: 8 to 10 servings

Candy Corn Snack Mix

1 BAG CANDY CORN

1 SMALL JAR SALTED PEANUTS

1 BOX RAISINS

Combine all ingredients in a bowl. Serve.
Yield: 4 to 6 servings

Almond Crunch Mix

1 (17.6 OUNCE) PACKAGE RICE SQUARES CEREAL

2¾ CUPS ALMONDS

1 CUP SUGAR

1 CUP LIGHT CORN SYRUP

¾ CUP BUTTER

1 TEASPOON ALMOND EXTRACT

Mix cereal and almonds in a large bowl; set aside. In a large saucepan, combine sugar, corn syrup, and butter; bring to a boil, stirring occasionally, until candy thermometer reads 250°. Remove from heat. Stir in almond extract. Pour over cereal mixture and mix well. Spread onto baking sheets lined with waxed paper to cool. Toss to break apart. Store in an airtight container.

Yield: 8 to 10 servings

Yummy Peanut Butter Balls

½ CUP CRISP RICE CEREAL

¼ CUP CREAMY PEANUT BUTTER

Combine cereal and peanut butter in a bowl, stirring well to coat cereal. Form mixture into balls. Place on waxed paper and freeze for 10 minutes or until hardened. Serve.

Yield: 2 servings

Frozen Fruit Snack

1¼ CUPS STRAWBERRIES

1 CUP SEEDLESS GRAPES

3 BANANAS, CUT INTO CUBES

1 CUP WATER

½ CAN FROZEN ORANGE JUICE CONCENTRATE

Combine all ingredients in a blender. Blend until smooth. Pour into small paper cups and freeze. Serve partially defrosted.

Yield: 6 to 8 servings

If you're overworked and overstressed, take a time-out and do absolutely nothing all by yourself. Savor this time and let the Lord speak to your heart.

Strawberry Graham Snack

8 GRAHAM CRACKERS, BROKEN CROSSWISE INTO HALVES

½ CUP CREAM CHEESE

12 STRAWBERRIES, SLICED

Spread graham crackers evenly with cream cheese; top with strawberry slices.

Yield: 4 to 8 servings

Gooey Banana Crackers

10 BUTTER-FLAVORED CRACKERS

1 BANANA, THINLY SLICED

2 TEASPOONS HONEY

Top crackers with banana slices. Drizzle with honey.

Yield: 10 servings

Frozen Bananas

BANANAS

YOGURT

PEANUT BUTTER

Cut bananas in half crosswise and place them on a tray in the freezer. When

frozen, place bananas in a plastic bag and keep frozen until ready to use.

Put yogurt and peanut butter in separate small bowls. Dip frozen banana

in toppings before each bite. (Allow bananas to thaw slightly before eating

them.)

Yield: 1 banana per person

Sweet Fruit Dip

1 (8 OUNCE) PACKAGE CREAM CHEESE, SOFTENED

1 (7 OUNCE) JAR MARSHMALLOW CRÈME

Beat cream cheese with hand mixer until creamy. Add marshmallow crème and whip until mixed well. Refrigerate. Serve with fruit of your choice.

Yield: 6 to 8 servings

For a tasty treat, try these dips on graham crackers, too. The combinations are delicious!

Apple Dip

1 (8 OUNCE) PACKAGE CREAM CHEESE, SOFTENED

BROWN SUGAR TO TASTE

VANILLA TO TASTE

Combine all ingredients and mix well. Serve with apple wedges.

Yield: 6 to 8 servings

Spinach Dip

1 ENVELOPE DRY ONION SOUP MIX
1 (16 OUNCE) CONTAINER SOUR CREAM
1 PACKAGE FROZEN CHOPPED SPINACH, THAWED AND DRAINED

Combine all ingredients. Refrigerate for 2 hours before serving. Serve with

veggies of your choice.

Yield: 8 to 10 servings

*Make your kitchen kid-friendly by stocking up
on plastic measuring cups, spoons, and mixing
bowls. Personalize them with a permanent
marker. Your children will love using their
own kitchen tools when they help
you prepare snacks and meals.*

Cucumber Spread

1 CUCUMBER, CHOPPED

1 SMALL ONION, CHOPPED

1 (8 OUNCE) PACKAGE CREAM CHEESE, SOFTENED

Place cucumber and onion in a blender or food processor; puree. Drain most of the juice from the vegetables through a strainer, then blend the vegetables into the cream cheese. Refrigerate for at least 12 hours. Serve on crackers or party rye bread.

Yield: 2 cups

For a nifty blender cleanup, fill $1/3$ of the blender with hot water. Add a drop of dish detergent. Cover and turn on for a few seconds. Rinse and dry.

Taco Dip

1 POUND GROUND BEEF

SALT AND PEPPER TO TASTE

1 (4 OUNCE) CAN DICED GREEN CHILIES

1 (14 TO 16 OUNCE) JAR TACO SAUCE

2½ CUPS CHEDDAR CHEESE, SHREDDED

In a skillet, brown ground beef and season with salt and pepper; drain. Add remaining ingredients. Heat until cheese melts, stirring occasionally. Serve with tortilla chips.

Yield: 6 to 8 servings

Place dips like this one in a small Crock-Pot to keep warm while serving to party guests.

Simple Salsa

2 (16 OUNCE) CANS DICED TOMATOES

1 TEASPOON CUMIN

1 TEASPOON SEASONED SALT

½ TEASPOON LIME JUICE

½ ONION

1 (4 OUNCE) CAN DICED GREEN CHILIES

½ TEASPOON GARLIC POWDER

½ GREEN BELL PEPPER

½ JALAPENO PEPPER

Place all ingredients in a blender and process quickly until vegetables are chopped. Refrigerate for 2½ hours to allow flavors to blend. Serve with tortilla chips.

Yield: 2 cups

Did you know lemons and limes can be frozen whole? Then when you're in need of fruit juice, you can simply thaw the lemon or lime in the microwave and squeeze out fresh-tasting juice any time of the year.

Only Martha takes the time for freshly squeezed lemon and lime juice! If you're like me, you'll simplify your life by purchasing the bottled juice at the supermarket.

Veggie Dip

1 CUP SOUR CREAM

2 DASHES HOT SAUCE

1 TABLESPOON PARSLEY FLAKES

½ TEASPOON GARLIC SALT

1 CUP MAYONNAISE

1 TABLESPOON HERB MIX

1 TEASPOON SEASONED SALT

Mix all ingredients well. Refrigerate for 2 hours to allow flavors to blend. Serve with veggies of your choice.

Yield: 2 cups

If you're like most busy women these days, you barely have time to yourself between work, running from here to there and back again with the kids, piles of laundry, and those 101 other things you need to accomplish all in 24 hours' time. When you're feeling stressed, recite the following verse and feel the tension melt away!

"Peace I leave with you; my peace I give you. I do not give to you as the world gives. Do not let your hearts be troubled."

JOHN 14:27

"It's So Easy!" Veggie Dip

1 (16 OUNCE) CONTAINER SOUR CREAM

1 ENVELOPE DRY ITALIAN DRESSING MIX

Combine sour cream and dressing mix. Cover and refrigerate for several hours to achieve best taste. Serve with veggies of your choice.

Yield: 2 cups

Cheesy Cracker Snack

1 CUP PROVOLONE CHEESE, SHREDDED

4 TABLESPOONS RED BELL PEPPER, FINELY CHOPPED

4 TABLESPOONS GREEN BELL PEPPER, FINELY CHOPPED

4 TABLESPOONS YELLOW BELL PEPPER, FINELY CHOPPED

30 CRACKERS

Combine cheese and peppers. Spoon evenly onto crackers. Place on a microwave-safe plate and microwave on HIGH for 10 to 15 seconds or just until cheese begins to melt.

Yield: 10 servings

Quick Cheesy Fries

1 (32 OUNCE) BAG FROZEN FRENCH FRIES

1 CAN CONDENSED CHEDDAR CHEESE SOUP

Bake French fries according to package directions. Spoon soup evenly over French fries, then bake for an additional 3 minutes.

Yield: 6 servings

Nachos 'n' Cheese with Salsa

TORTILLA CHIPS

PROCESSED CHEESE SLICES

SALSA

Place desired amount of tortilla chips on baking sheet. Top with processed cheese slices. Place in 250° oven and heat until cheese melts. Serve with salsa.

Yield: Customizable

Dill Pickle Fryers

1 CUP FLOUR

¼ TEASPOON SALT

1 EGG

½ CUP MILK

1½ CUPS DILL PICKLE SLICES, DRAINED

VEGETABLE OIL

Combine flour and salt in a shallow mixing bowl. In a separate bowl, beat eggs and milk. Remove excess moisture from pickle slices by blotting with a paper towel. Coat pickles with flour mixture, dip in egg mixture, then dip in flour mixture one more time. In a deep skillet, heat oil to 375°. Fry pickles for approximately 3 minutes or until golden brown, turning once during frying. Drain. Serve with ranch dressing if desired.

Yield: 2 to 4 servings

Whoever would have thought to fry pickles? What a surprise your party guests will have biting into this zesty appetizer!

Cracker Sandwiches

12 BUTTER-FLAVORED CRACKERS

2 TABLESPOONS MAYONNAISE

2 SLICES AMERICAN CHEESE

2 SLICES BOLOGNA

1 LARGE PLUM TOMATO, CUT INTO 6 SLICES

Spread crackers with mayonnaise. Cut cheese and bologna slices to fit onto the crackers; place one slice of cheese and one slice of bologna on each of 6 crackers. Top each with 1 tomato slice. Top with remaining crackers to form sandwiches.

Yield: 6 servings

Quick Club Quesadillas

8 SLICES BACON, COOKED

8 SLICES DELI TURKEY BREAST

4 LARGE FLOUR TORTILLAS

2 TOMATOES, CHOPPED

1 CUP SHREDDED LETTUCE

½ CUP MONTEREY JACK CHEESE, SHREDDED

¼ CUP RANCH DRESSING

Place 2 bacon slices and 2 turkey slices in center of each tortilla. Top with tomatoes, lettuce, and cheese. Fold in half. Cook each tortilla in a skillet on medium heat for 3 minutes on each side or until crispy and golden brown. Cut tortilla into wedges. Serve each quesadilla with 1 tablespoon ranch dressing.

Yield: 4 servings

OUT THE DOOR
IN A FLASH

Meals on the Go

*It matters not how simple the food—a chop, steak, or a plain boiled
or roast joint, but let it be of good quality and properly cooked,
and everyone who partakes of it will enjoy it.*

ALEXIS SOYER (1809–1858), French chef

Amish Peanut Butter Spread

1 QUART MAPLE-FLAVORED PANCAKE SYRUP

2 CUPS CREAMY PEANUT BUTTER

1 CUP MARSHMALLOW CRÈME

Blend all ingredients well. Store in an airtight jar. Ready to use immediately on bread or toast.

Yield: 7 cups

Tuna Cheese Spread

1 (8 OUNCE) PACKAGE CREAM CHEESE, SOFTENED

1 (6 OUNCE) CAN TUNA, DRAINED AND FLAKED

½ CUP GREEN ONION, FINELY CHOPPED

¼ CUP MAYONNAISE

1 TABLESPOON LEMON JUICE

¾ TEASPOON CURRY POWDER

DASH SALT

Combine all ingredients. Spread onto bread slices for quick, tasty sandwiches.

Yield: 2 cups

Quiet my soul, Lord. Help me to lay my worries and stresses at Your feet and focus on enjoying time with my family. Remind me that it's okay to cut out the unnecessary tasks today and to leave some things for tomorrow. Amen.

Cast all your anxiety on him because he cares for you.

1 PETER 5:7

Vineyard Chicken Salad

1 POUND BONELESS, SKINLESS CHICKEN BREASTS, COOKED AND FINELY CHOPPED

1 CUP MAYONNAISE

1 CUP GRAPES, QUARTERED

½ CUP DATES, CHOPPED

1 SMALL CAN CRUSHED PINEAPPLE, DRAINED

1 STALK CELERY, FINELY CHOPPED

1 TO 1½ TEASPOONS ALL SEASON (LOW SALT)

Combine all ingredients in a large bowl, adding more mayonnaise if mixture is too dry. Chill for 2 hours to allow flavors to blend. Serve on bread, croissants, or crackers.

Yield: 8 servings

Classic Egg Salad

6 EGGS

1 TABLESPOON SALAD DRESSING OR MAYONNAISE

2 TEASPOONS MUSTARD

2 TEASPOONS VINEGAR

½ TEASPOON SALT

DASH PEPPER

In a medium saucepan, cover eggs with cold water. Put lid on the pan. Bring eggs to a boil, then immediately turn heat to low. If eggs cook too hard, they will crack. Boil for 12 to 15 minutes, depending on the size of the eggs. Remove eggs from boiling water and cool. Peel eggs, place them in a bowl, and mash them with a fork. Add salad dressing, mustard, vinegar, salt, and pepper. Mix well. Place a piece of lettuce on a slice of bread, add egg salad, and cover with another slice of bread. Cut diagonally, and you have an attractive lunch.

Yield: 4 to 6 servings

When boiling eggs, I add a tablespoon of vinegar to the water to keep the eggs from cooking out if they crack. Also, remove from heat immediately and add cold water to the pan to cool them quickly. They will peel more easily.

Egg Salad with a Twist
Sandwich Spread

6 HARD-BOILED EGGS, CHOPPED

¼ CUP CARROTS, SHREDDED

2 TABLESPOONS CELERY, FINELY CHOPPED

1 TABLESPOON GREEN ONION, FINELY CHOPPED

¼ CUP CREAM CHEESE, SOFTENED

2 TABLESPOONS MAYONNAISE

¼ TEASPOON SEASONED SALT

¼ TEASPOON DILL WEED

PINCH DRY MUSTARD

PINCH SALT

PINCH PEPPER

Combine eggs, carrots, celery, and green onion in a bowl; set aside. Mix cream cheese, mayonnaise, and seasonings until thoroughly blended. Combine cream cheese mixture and egg mixture. Cover and refrigerate until ready to use.

Yield: 6 servings

Mini Pizza Delights

1 ENGLISH MUFFIN, SLICED IN HALF

TOMATO SAUCE (OR PIZZA SAUCE)

MOZZARELLA CHEESE, SHREDDED

**TOPPINGS OF YOUR CHOICE
(PEPPERONI, MUSHROOMS, ONION, GREEN PEPPER)**

Top English muffin halves with tomato sauce, cheese, and toppings of your

choice. Cook in microwave oven until cheese is melted.

Yield: 2 servings

*Make your kids mini "message" pizzas. Use
toppings to create words. For example, take
chopped green pepper and place it so it spells
"love you." Or create a personalized pizza
by making an initial with mushrooms. Your
children will look forward to the next special
pizza you create just for them!*

Baked Pizza Sandwich

2 TABLESPOONS BUTTER, SOFTENED

1½ TEASPOONS ITALIAN SEASONING

1 TEASPOON MINCED GARLIC

**1 (16 OUNCE) PREPARED ITALIAN BREAD SHELL,
SLICED IN HALF HORIZONTALLY**

4 OUNCES SANDWICH PEPPERONI

4 GREEN BELL PEPPER RINGS

4 TOMATO SLICES

6 SLICES PROVOLONE CHEESE

Combine butter, Italian seasoning, and garlic in a small bowl. Spread mixture on one half of bread shell. Layer with pepperoni, green pepper, tomato, and cheese. Top with remaining half of bread shell. Wrap in aluminum foil and place on a baking sheet. Bake at 350° for 18 minutes or until cheese is melted. Cut into 4 sections and serve warm.

Yield: 4 servings

Apple–Peanut Butter Bagel Sandwiches

1 WHEAT BAGEL, SPLIT

4 TEASPOONS PEANUT BUTTER

2 SLICES AMERICAN CHEESE

6 SLICES RED APPLE

Spread 2 teaspoons peanut butter on cut side of each bagel half. Top with cheese slice and apple slices.

Yield: 2 servings

Best Turkey Bagel

1 WHEAT OR PLAIN BAGEL

2 SLICES MONTEREY JACK CHEESE

2 SLICES CUCUMBER

3 SLICES DELI TURKEY

RANCH DRESSING

Toast the split bagel. Layer one half with cheese and cucumber. Top with turkey.

Add ranch dressing as desired. Top with other half of bagel.

Yield: 1 serving

Toasty Ham Salad Sandwiches

½ PINT DELI HAM SALAD

6 MINI BAKERY BUNS

6 SLICES AMERICAN CHEESE

Spread 2 tablespoons ham salad onto bottom half of each bun. Layer with

cheese and top of bun. Place sandwiches in a 9x13-inch baking pan; cover with

aluminum foil. Bake at 350° for 20 minutes or until heated through. Serve warm.

Yield: 6 servings

Fried Bologna Sandwich

1 SLICE BOLOGNA

2 SLICES BREAD

CONDIMENTS OF YOUR CHOICE

Cut a slit in the center of the bologna slice to help it lie flat. Spray the bottom of a small skillet with oil. Brown meat over medium heat. Turn once. Place fried bologna between bread slices. Add mustard or ketchup if desired. You may want to try adding some barbecue green tomato relish.

Yield: 1 serving

Pigs in a Blanket

1 TUBE REFRIGERATED CRESCENT ROLL DOUGH

8 HOT DOGS

Separate triangles of dough and place them on a lightly greased cookie sheet.
Wrap each triangle of dough around a hot dog and seal as much as possible.
Bake at 350° for 10 minutes or until bread is golden brown. You can wrap a
small strip of cheese with the hot dog if desired.

Yield: 8 servings

Burrito Wraps

1 CAN CONDENSED CHILI

6 LARGE FLOUR TORTILLAS

MONTEREY JACK/COLBY CHEESE, SHREDDED

Place 2 tablespoons of chili in center of tortillas. Top with cheese. Wrap tortilla
around filling. Place folded side down on microwave-safe plate and cook on
HIGH for 2 minutes.

Yield: 6 servings

Salsa-Potato Burritos

1 (16 OUNCE) PACKAGE FROZEN HASH BROWNS

1 CUP SALSA

2 CUPS CHEDDAR CHEESE, SHREDDED

6 LARGE FLOUR TORTILLAS

Cook hash browns according to package directions. Add salsa and cheese; sauté for 3 minutes or until hot. Fold into warmed flour tortillas.

Yield: 6 servings

Designate one evening each week as "music night." Take turns letting each family member choose music to accompany your meal. Even if you're not particularly fond of the music choice, be sure to appreciate each other's differences.

Ham 'n' Cheese Rolls

2 (10 OUNCE) TUBES REFRIGERATED PIZZA DOUGH
½ POUND DELI HAM, THINLY SLICED
8 SLICES SWISS CHEESE

Unroll each rectangle of pizza dough on lightly floured surface; cut dough into quarters to make 8 small rectangles. Press each quarter of dough into a 7x4-inch rectangle. On each section of dough, layer an eighth of the ham and 1 cheese slice to within ½ inch of edge. Roll up dough, starting with the short end; seal edges well. Place sandwiches on greased baking sheet, seam side down. Bake for 14 minutes or until golden brown.

Yield: 8 servings

Yummy Grilled Cheese

2 SLICES TEXAS TOAST

MAYONNAISE (NO SUBSTITUTES)

1 SLICE AMERICAN CHEESE

Heat a small skillet over medium heat. Spread mayonnaise onto one slice of the bread, then place mayonnaise side down in skillet. Top with cheese. Spread mayonnaise onto second slice of bread, then place mayonnaise side up on top of cheese. Cook for 3 minutes on each side or until bread is golden brown.

Yield: 1 serving

Don't use a salad dressing like Miracle Whip for this sandwich; the sugar in it tends to burn.

Anytime Egg Fajitas

2 TABLESPOONS VEGETABLE OIL

2 CUPS FROZEN HASH BROWNS

½ POUND SPICY BULK SAUSAGE

5 EGGS

½ CUP GREEN BELL PEPPER, CHOPPED

¼ CUP ONION, CHOPPED

1 CUP CHEDDAR CHEESE, SHREDDED

8 LARGE FLOUR TORTILLAS

Heat oil in a large skillet. Add hash browns and cook over medium heat, stirring constantly until lightly browned. Add sausage and stir frequently until sausage is thoroughly cooked. Beat eggs in a small bowl and add to hash brown mixture along with green pepper and onion. Cook, stirring occasionally, until eggs are set and thoroughly cooked. Microwave tortillas on HIGH for 25 to 30 seconds to soften. Spoon egg mixture onto center of softened tortillas and top with cheese. Roll up tortillas.

Yield: 8 servings

Mexican Sandwich Rolls

3 POUNDS GROUND BEEF

1 MEDIUM ONION, CHOPPED

3 CUPS CHEDDAR CHEESE, GRATED

1 (15 OUNCE) CAN TOMATO SAUCE

1 (4 OUNCE) JAR SALSA

2 DOZEN HARD ROLLS

Brown ground beef and onion; drain. Add remaining ingredients, except rolls.

Remove a pinch of bread from center of rolls, then fill with beef mixture.

Wrap each in foil. Bake at 350° for 30 minutes.

Yield: 24 rolls

To thaw meat at room temperature,
place it on a metal pan. Metal conducts heat.

Corned Beef Sandwich

1 (12 OUNCE) CAN CORNED BEEF

2 SMALL ONIONS, FINELY CHOPPED

4 STALKS CELERY, FINELY CHOPPED

4 TEASPOONS MAYONNAISE

½ POUND PROCESSED CHEESE, CUT INTO SMALL CUBES

12 BUNS

Combine first five ingredients, fill buns, and wrap each bun in foil. Heat sandwiches at 350° for 15 minutes.

Yield: 12 servings

Family-Size Gyro

1 (8 INCH) LOAF ROUND BREAD, UNSLICED

½ CUP BUTTER

4 OUNCES ROAST BEEF, THINLY SLICED

8 SLICES AMERICAN CHEESE

¼ CUP THOUSAND ISLAND DRESSING

6 LETTUCE LEAVES

1 MEDIUM TOMATO, SLICED

4 OUNCES PASTRAMI, THINLY SLICED

16 SLICES MONTEREY JACK CHEESE

Cut bread loaf horizontally into 4 slices. Spread all cut surfaces with butter.
Place bottom slice of loaf on platter; top with roast beef and American cheese.
Top with 2 tablespoons Thousand Island dressing. Place second bread slice
on top of beef and cheese; top with lettuce and tomato. Place third bread
slice on top of tomato; top with pastrami and Monterey Jack cheese. Top with
remaining Thousand Island dressing. Add remaining bread slice. Cut into 8
wedges.

Yield: 8 servings

Cheesy Chicken Potatoes

4 LARGE POTATOES

2 TABLESPOONS VEGETABLE OIL

2 BONELESS, SKINLESS CHICKEN BREASTS, CUT INTO CHUNKS

1 CUP BROCCOLI FLORETS

1 CAN CONDENSED CHEDDAR CHEESE SOUP

Cook potatoes in microwave until done (approximately 4 to 6 minutes per potato on HIGH). Place vegetable oil and chicken in skillet and cook until chicken is browned; add broccoli florets. Cook 5 minutes over medium-high heat. Place baked potatoes on a microwave-safe plate. Cut open and fluff potatoes with fork. Top with broccoli and chicken. Spoon cheese soup over top. Microwave on HIGH for 4 minutes.

Yield: 4 servings

MIX IT ALL TOGETHER— & VOILÁ!

Casseroles & Other One-Dish Wonders

Our life is frittered away by detail. . . . Simplify, simplify.

HENRY DAVID THOREAU (1817–1862), American author and philosopher

Country Breakfast Casserole

½ **POUND SPICY BULK PORK SAUSAGE**

½ **CUP ONION, FINELY CHOPPED**

4 **CUPS DICED HASH BROWN POTATOES**

1½ **CUPS COLBY/MONTEREY JACK CHEESE, SHREDDED**

3 **EGGS, BEATEN**

1 **CUP MILK**

¼ **TEASPOON PEPPER**

SALSA

In a large skillet, brown sausage and onion; drain. In an 8-inch square baking dish, layer potatoes, half of cheese, sausage mixture, and remaining cheese. Combine eggs, milk, and pepper; pour over cheese. Bake, uncovered, at 350° for 50 to 55 minutes or until a knife inserted near center comes out clean. Let stand for 10 minutes. Slice into squares and serve with salsa.

Yield: 4 servings

I despise cleaning up my food processor, so I don't use it very often. When I have it out, I chop or grate several vegetables at once. Chopped celery, green pepper, and onion can then be stored in tightly sealed bags in the freezer until I need them for a recipe.

Sausage 'n' Cheese Grits Casserole

4 CUPS WATER

1 TEASPOON SALT

1 CUP QUICK GRITS

4 EGGS, BEATEN

1 POUND SAUSAGE, BROWNED

1½ CUPS CHEDDAR CHEESE, SHREDDED AND DIVIDED

1 CUP MILK

½ CUP MARGARINE

Grease a 3-quart baking dish and set aside. Bring water and salt to a boil in a large saucepan. Slowly stir in grits; cook for 4 to 5 minutes, stirring occasionally. Remove from heat. Stir grits mixture into eggs; return all to saucepan. Add sausage, 1 cup of cheese, milk, and margarine; blend well. Pour into a baking dish, then sprinkle with remaining cheese. Bake at 350° for approximately 1 hour. Let stand for 10 minutes before serving.

Yield: 6 servings

Chicken 'n' Corn Bread Casserole

¼ CUP MARGARINE

1 SMALL ONION, CHOPPED

2 STALKS CELERY, CHOPPED

1 CUP FLOUR, DIVIDED

1 TEASPOON SALT

⅛ TEASPOON DRIED ROSEMARY

2⅔ CUPS MILK, DIVIDED

1 CUP CHICKEN BROTH

2½ CUPS CHICKEN, COOKED AND CUBED

½ CUP CORNMEAL

1 TABLESPOON SUGAR

1½ TABLESPOONS BAKING POWDER

½ TEASPOON SALT

1 EGG

3 TABLESPOONS VEGETABLE OIL

In a skillet, heat margarine and sauté onion and celery. Sprinkle ½ cup flour over contents of the skillet and blend into the margarine. Season with salt and rosemary. Over low heat, slowly blend 2 cups milk into the margarine. Add broth, stirring constantly until mixture thickens. Add chicken and pour all into a 7x12-inch baking dish. Sift together cornmeal, ½ cup flour, sugar, baking powder, and salt. In a separate dish, beat egg, then stir in ⅔ cup milk and oil. Blend egg mixture into sifted mixture. Pour over chicken mixture and bake at 425° for 20 minutes or until browned.

Yield: 6 servings

Chicken 'n' Wild Rice Casserole

3 CUPS COOKED CHICKEN, CUBED

2½ CUPS WILD RICE, COOKED

1 CAN CONDENSED CREAM OF CHICKEN SOUP

1 CAN CONDENSED CREAM OF MUSHROOM SOUP

1 CUP MILK

1 (6 OUNCE) CAN SLICED MUSHROOMS, DRAINED

½ CUP ONION, FINELY CHOPPED

½ CUP GREEN BELL PEPPER, CHOPPED

Combine all ingredients and pour into a large casserole dish. Bake at 350° for 45 minutes.

Yield: 4 to 6 servings

*9/29/09 –
Sammi –
good – not great –
Sammi did
AOK!*

Tuna Noodle Casserole

1 CAN CONDENSED CREAM OF MUSHROOM SOUP

½ CUP MILK

1 CUP PEAS, COOKED

2 (6 OUNCE) CANS TUNA, DRAINED AND FLAKED

2 CUPS EGG NOODLES, COOKED

2 TABLESPOONS DRY BREAD CRUMBS

1 TABLESPOON MARGARINE, MELTED

Mix soup, milk, peas, tuna, and egg noodles in a 1½-quart casserole dish. Bake at 400° for 20 minutes. Stir. Mix bread crumbs with margarine and sprinkle on top of casserole. Bake an additional 5 minutes before serving.

Yield: 4 to 6 servings

Encourage your kids to help out with meal preparation. As they're measuring ingredients and having fun with you in the kitchen, they're also learning fractions (and they won't even realize it!).

Crisp Rice Casserole

2 CUPS WATER

1 CUP RICE, UNCOOKED

3 CUPS CRISP RICE CEREAL, DIVIDED

1 POUND SAUSAGE

1 SMALL ONION, CHOPPED

2 CUPS CHEDDAR CHEESE, SHREDDED

3 EGGS

2 CANS CONDENSED CREAM OF CELERY SOUP

MILK

In a medium saucepan, bring water to a boil. Add rice, cover, and cook over low heat for 20 minutes. Grease a 7x12-inch baking dish and cover the bottom with 2 cups of cereal. Brown sausage and onion; drain and layer over cereal. Top with cooked rice and cheese. In a bowl, beat eggs and blend in soup and half a soup can of milk. Pour egg mixture over cheese, poking a few holes down through the layers to allow egg mixture to soak through. Add 2 cups cereal on top. Bake at 400° for 30 to 40 minutes or until bubbly.

Yield: 4 servings

Cheesy Noodle Casserole

1 (16 OUNCE) PACKAGE EGG NOODLES

¼ CUP BUTTER

⅛ CUP FLOUR

½ TEASPOON GARLIC SALT

½ TEASPOON ONION SALT

3 CUPS MILK

1 POUND PROCESSED CHEESE, CUBED

TOPPING:

¼ CUP BREAD CRUMBS

1 TABLESPOON BUTTER, MELTED

Cook noodles according to package directions. Melt butter in medium saucepan; add flour, garlic salt, and onion salt, stirring after each addition. Gradually add milk; stir thoroughly. Bring to a boil. Cook and stir for 2 minutes or until mixture thickens. Add cheese and stir until melted. Add noodles. Pour into a greased 2-quart baking dish. Toss bread crumbs in melted butter and sprinkle over top of casserole. Bake, uncovered, at 350° for 25 minutes or until golden brown.

Yield: 6 to 8 servings

Do you find that you spend too much time worrying about what you just have to get done? Intentionally redirect your thoughts toward gratitude. What are you most thankful for? Your health? A loving family? A great career? You'll quickly forget about your worries when you see how richly the Lord has blessed you.

Give thanks to the LORD, for he is good.

PSALM 136:1

Lolita's Summer Zucchini Casserole

⅓ CUP OLIVE OIL

2 TABLESPOONS WHITE WINE VINEGAR

2 TABLESPOONS PARSLEY

3 TEASPOONS SALT

¾ TEASPOON PEPPER

1 TEASPOON HOT SAUCE

1 MEDIUM ZUCCHINI, CHOPPED

2 WHITE POTATOES, CHOPPED

2 SMALL GREEN BELL PEPPERS, CHOPPED

2 CARROTS, CHOPPED

1 CELERY STALK, CHOPPED

3 TO 4 MEDIUM TOMATOES, THINLY SLICED

⅓ TO ½ CUP RAW RICE (NOT INSTANT)

1¾ CUPS CHEDDAR CHEESE, SHREDDED

Blend oil, vinegar, parsley, salt, pepper, and hot sauce; set aside. In a large bowl, combine zucchini, potatoes, green pepper, carrots, and celery. Spray a large casserole dish with oil. Cover bottom with sliced tomatoes (saving some for top layers). Cover with half of the vegetables. Add another layer of tomatoes. Sprinkle with rice. Add remaining vegetables and top with a final layer of tomatoes. Stir oil mixture and pour over all. Cover with foil and bake at 350° for 1 hour and 25 minutes. Remove foil and sprinkle casserole with cheese. Bake for an additional 15 minutes.

Yield: 8 servings

This is a wonderful, colorful combination of garden produce in a scrumptious veggie casserole that everyone will rave over.

9/26/09-

45-Minute Casserole

1 POUND GROUND BEEF

1 LARGE ONION, CHOPPED

1 CAN CONDENSED CREAM OF CELERY SOUP

1 SMALL CAN SAUERKRAUT

1 BAG FROZEN TATER TOTS

Brown ground beef and onion; drain. Place in a casserole dish. Top with soup.

Drain and rinse sauerkraut; spread over casserole mixture. Place tater tots over

all. Bake at 350° for 45 minutes.

Yield: 4 servings

I like to be sure I drain all the fat off my ground beef after it's cooked, but it's hard to pour or spoon it all off without getting the meat mixed in. To soak up any remaining grease, dab cooked beef with a stale piece of bread or a bread heel.

Beefy Noodle Casserole

1 POUND GROUND BEEF

1 (16 OUNCE) PACKAGE EGG NOODLES

1 CAN CONDENSED CREAM OF MUSHROOM SOUP

½ CUP MILK

5 TABLESPOONS BUTTER

SALT AND PEPPER TO TASTE

Brown ground beef; drain. Cook noodles according to package directions; drain. Combine all ingredients in a large casserole dish. Bake at 350° for 30 minutes.

Yield: 4 servings

10/13/09

Ham 'n' Potato Casserole

3 (16 OUNCE) PACKAGES FROZEN HASH BROWNS

3 (8 OUNCE) PACKAGES CHEDDAR CHEESE, SHREDDED

2 POUNDS HAM, DICED

2 CANS CONDENSED CHEDDAR CHEESE SOUP

2 ONIONS, DICED

1 QUART MILK

Mix all ingredients in large roaster pan. Bake at 400° for 1 hour. Stir

occasionally while baking.

Yield: 8 to 10 servings

Make cleanup a snap by washing your pots and pans as soon as you're finished with them. The longer you let them sit, the harder it will be to get them clean and the more time you'll have to spend in the kitchen (when you could be out there enjoying life!).

Fiesta Casserole

1½ POUNDS GROUND BEEF

1 ENVELOPE TACO SEASONING

1 (15 OUNCE) CAN TOMATO SAUCE

1 (11 OUNCE) CAN WHOLE-KERNEL CORN, DRAINED

1 CUP CHEDDAR CHEESE, SHREDDED

1 CUP TORTILLA CHIPS, COARSELY CRUSHED

SOUR CREAM

1 TOMATO, CHOPPED

½ HEAD LETTUCE, CHOPPED

Brown ground beef in a large skillet; drain. Stir in taco seasoning, tomato sauce, and corn. Simmer for 5 minutes. Spoon mixture into a 2-quart baking dish.

Top with cheese and crushed tortilla chips. Bake at 250° until cheese is melted, approximately 6 to 10 minutes. Garnish with sour cream and top with tomato and lettuce.

Yield: 4 to 6 servings

Taco Plate

CHICKEN (OR GROUND BEEF), COOKED AND SHREDDED
TACO SEASONING
LETTUCE
CHEESE, SHREDDED
SALSA
SOUR CREAM
TORTILLA CHIPS

Place chicken in a saucepan or skillet, sprinkle with taco seasoning, and add a little water to cover the bottom of the pan. Heat to a boil and stir until water is cooked away. Cover the bottom of a plate with shredded lettuce; top with layers of seasoned chicken, cheese, salsa, and sour cream to your taste. Serve with tortilla chips.

Yield: Easily adjusted from 1 to several servings

Super-Easy Chicken Pot Pie

1 CAN CONDENSED CREAM OF CHICKEN SOUP

1 (9 OUNCE) PACKAGE FROZEN MIXED VEGETABLES, THAWED

1 CUP CHICKEN, COOKED AND CUBED

1¼ CUPS ALL-PURPOSE BAKING MIX

½ CUP MILK

1 EGG

Mix soup, vegetables, and chicken in a 9-inch pie plate. In a separate bowl, mix milk, egg, and baking mix; pour over chicken mixture. Bake at 400° for 30 minutes or until golden brown.

Yield: 4 servings

Curried Honey Chicken

¼ CUP BUTTER

1 CUP HONEY

¼ CUP DIJON MUSTARD

2 TEASPOONS CURRY POWDER

1 TEASPOON SALT

1½ POUNDS BONELESS, SKINLESS CHICKEN BREASTS, CUT INTO CHUNKS

In a saucepan, melt butter and whisk in honey, mustard, curry, and salt. Add chicken and stir to coat. Place chicken mixture in a 2-quart baking dish. Bake at 375° for 45 minutes, basting occasionally. Chicken will be golden when done. Serve over hot cooked rice.

Yield: 4 servings

Chicken Waikiki

1 WHOLE CHICKEN, CUT UP

1 TEASPOON SALT

¼ TEASPOON PEPPER

½ CUP FLOUR

⅓ CUP CANOLA OIL

1 (20 OUNCE) CAN PINEAPPLE SLICES

1 CUP SUGAR

2 TABLESPOONS CORNSTARCH

¾ CUP CIDER VINEGAR

1 TABLESPOON SOY SAUCE

¼ TEASPOON GROUND GINGER

1 CHICKEN BOUILLON CUBE

1 LARGE GREEN BELL PEPPER, SLICED

Sprinkle each piece of chicken with salt and pepper, dredge in flour, then brown in hot oil. Transfer browned chicken to a roasting pan. Drain pineapple into a 2-cup measuring cup. Add enough water to juice to equal 1¼ cups liquid. In a saucepan, combine sugar, cornstarch, pineapple juice, vinegar, soy sauce, ginger, and bouillon. Bring liquid to a boil and boil for 2 minutes. Pour sauce over chicken. Bake, uncovered, at 350° for 30 minutes. Add slices of pineapple and green pepper, and bake for an additional 30 minutes. Serve over hot cooked rice.

Yield: 4 servings

Home-Style Sausage, Cabbage, and Potatoes

4 POTATOES, PEELED AND CUT INTO ¼-INCH CHUNKS

½ MEDIUM ONION, SLICED

2 CUPS CABBAGE, CUT INTO LARGE CHUNKS

1 POUND SMOKED SAUSAGE OR HAM, CUT INTO CHUNKS

½ TEASPOON SALT

¼ TEASPOON PEPPER

1 CUP WATER

Combine all ingredients in a large saucepan. Bring to a boil. Cover and cook over low heat for 15 to 25 minutes or until potatoes are tender.

Yield: 4 to 6 servings

Before peeling new potatoes, soak them in cold salted water for 30 minutes. They will peel more easily and won't stain your hands.

Grandma Shutt's Meat Loaf

4 POUNDS GROUND BEEF

1⅓ CUP OATS, UNCOOKED

⅔ CUP ONION, CHOPPED

2 TEASPOONS SALT

½ TEASPOON PEPPER

2 CUPS TOMATO JUICE

2 EGGS, BEATEN

Combine all ingredients; mix thoroughly. Pack firmly into an ungreased loaf pan.

Bake at 350° for 1 hour and 15 minutes. Let stand for 5 minutes before serving.

Yield: 8 to 10 servings

Hash

1 TO 2 TABLESPOONS CANOLA OIL

2 CUPS POTATOES, COOKED AND CUBED

1 CUP BEEF ROAST, COOKED AND CHOPPED

2 TABLESPOONS ONION, CHOPPED

2 TABLESPOONS GREEN BELL PEPPER, CHOPPED (OPTIONAL)

1 TABLESPOON WORCESTERSHIRE SAUCE

2 EGGS

SALT AND PEPPER

Heat oil in a skillet. Add potatoes, beef roast, onion, and green pepper to the skillet. Heat through, then blend in Worcestershire sauce, and break eggs over the mixture and stir with a spatula until eggs are set. Season with salt and pepper.

Yield: 2 servings

Hash has long been an easy way to use up leftovers in my house. It gives a simple roast with potatoes a completely renewed taste.

Cheesy Chicken Bake

5 BONELESS, SKINLESS CHICKEN BREASTS

1 CAN CONDENSED CREAM OF CHICKEN SOUP

5 SLICES AMERICAN CHEESE

BUTTER

GARLIC SALT

Place chicken in a shallow baking pan. Pour soup over chicken pieces, then top with cheese slices. Place a chunk of butter on each piece and sprinkle with garlic salt. Bake at 350° for 45 to 50 minutes. Serve over rice or noodles, if desired. Yield: 5 servings

Don't throw away your leftovers! Use leftover chicken, chili, beans, and more to create tasty burritos. Your family will love this tasty new twist, and you won't need to throw out your leftovers anymore.

Taco Bake

1 POUND GROUND BEEF

1 CAN CONDENSED TOMATO SOUP

1 CUP SALSA

½ CUP MILK

6 MEDIUM FLOUR TORTILLAS, CUT INTO 1-INCH STRIPS

1 CUP COLBY/MONTEREY JACK CHEESE, DIVIDED

Brown ground beef; drain. Add soup, salsa, milk, tortilla strips, and half of the cheese. Pour mixture into a 2-quart casserole dish and cover. Bake at 400° for 30 minutes. Remove from oven and sprinkle with remaining cheese before serving. Yield: 4 servings

Hawaiian Burgers

2 POUNDS GROUND BEEF

½ CUP HONEY

¼ TEASPOON CINNAMON

¼ TEASPOON CURRY POWDER

⅛ TEASPOON GROUND NUTMEG

⅛ TEASPOON GROUND GINGER

¼ CUP SOY SAUCE

1 (23 OUNCE) CAN PINEAPPLE SLICES, DRAINED

8 HAMBURGER BUNS

8 LETTUCE LEAVES

8 TOMATO SLICES

MAYONNAISE

In a mixing bowl, combine beef, honey, cinnamon, curry, nutmeg, and ginger. Shape into 8 patties. Grill burgers over medium heat for 3 minutes on each side. Baste with soy sauce. Grill 4 to 6 minutes longer, until juices run clear. Place pineapple slices on the grill during the end of the burgers' cooking time; turn once. Serve burgers on buns with pineapple, lettuce, tomato, and mayonnaise.

Yield: 8 servings

To make uniform hamburger patties, find a jar lid of the desired size and wash it well. Pack the lid tightly with ground beef, smooth the top with a knife, turn over, tap out the patty...and voilá! Beautifully shaped hamburgers!

Hamburger Gravy

½ TO 1 POUND GROUND BEEF

ONION OR ONION POWDER

GARLIC POWDER

2 TABLESPOONS CANOLA OIL

4 TABLESPOONS FLOUR

3 CUPS MILK

1 TEASPOON SALT

½ TEASPOON PEPPER

Brown ground beef in a large skillet; drain. Season with onion and/or a little garlic powder. Add oil and mix in flour to make a paste. Gradually add milk and stir over medium heat until mixture bubbles and thickens. Add more milk or water if it is too thick. If gravy is too thin, mix a little flour with cold water, add it to the gravy, and let it boil to thicken. Add salt and pepper. Stir well and serve over mashed potatoes, fried potatoes, biscuits, or bread.

Yield: 4 servings

Easy Beef Skillet

1 CUP POTATOES, SLICED

1 TABLESPOON CANOLA OIL

1 POUND GROUND BEEF

1 CAN CONDENSED TOMATO SOUP

¼ CUP WATER

1 TABLESPOON WORCESTERSHIRE SAUCE

⅓ TEASPOON PEPPER

1 (8 OUNCE) CAN CUT GREEN BEANS, DRAINED

Fry potatoes in oil over medium heat until soft. Remove from heat. Brown ground beef in a skillet over medium heat; drain. Add tomato soup, water, Worcestershire sauce, pepper, green beans, and cooked potatoes. Cook over low heat for 10 to 15 minutes or until heated through.

Yield: 4 servings

BBQ Hamburger Muffins

1 POUND GROUND BEEF

½ CUP ONION, FINELY CHOPPED

½ CUP BARBECUE SAUCE

GARLIC POWDER

1 (10 COUNT) TUBE REFRIGERATED BISCUITS

½ CUP CHEDDAR OR SWISS CHEESE, SHREDDED

Brown ground beef and onions; drain. Add barbecue sauce and garlic powder. Pull apart biscuits and place individual biscuits in muffin pan. Place meat mixture on top of biscuits. Bake at 375° for 15 to 20 minutes. Remove from oven and cover each hamburger muffin with cheese; bake an additional 5 minutes or until cheese is completely melted.

Yield: 10 servings

Take time in your day to be inspired by something small—the scent of a flower from your garden, a hug from a child, an "I love you" from your spouse.... Then thank God for the little things in life.

Enjoy the little things, for one day you may look back and discover they were the big things.

UNKNOWN

Tasty Baked Steak

3 POUNDS ROUND STEAK

2 TEASPOONS BUTTER

1 SMALL ONION, CUT INTO RINGS

1 CUP KETCHUP

1 TABLESPOON WORCESTERSHIRE SAUCE

⅓ CUP WATER

Place steak in a shallow baking pan. Spread butter over steak and top with onion. Mix ketchup, Worcestershire sauce, and water; pour over steak; cover. Bake at 350° for 2½ hours.

Yield: 4 servings

No-Peek Steak

4 POUNDS ROUND STEAK, CUT INTO SQUARES

1 CAN CONDENSED CREAM OF MUSHROOM SOUP

1 CAN CONDENSED CREAM OF CELERY SOUP

1 CAN CONDENSED CREAM OF ONION SOUP

1 CAN SLICED MUSHROOMS

Place steak in a casserole dish. Combine soups and pour over top of steak. Spread mushrooms over all. Bake at 225° for 4 hours. Don't peek!

Yield: 6 servings

Pepper Steak

1½ POUNDS ROUND STEAK

2 TABLESPOONS COOKING OIL

2 MEDIUM GREEN BELL PEPPERS,
   CUT INTO SHORT STRIPS

1 SMALL ONION, SLICED

2 MEDIUM TOMATOES,
   PEELED AND CHOPPED

1 CUP WATER

¼ CUP SOY SAUCE

½ TEASPOON PEPPER

¼ TEASPOON SALT

¼ TEASPOON GROUND GINGER

2 TABLESPOONS CORNSTARCH

2 TABLESPOONS WATER

4 CUPS RICE, COOKED

With a meat mallet, pound steak to ¼-inch thick, then cut steak across the grain into thin strips. In a large skillet, heat oil and brown steak on both sides; drain. Add green pepper, onion, and tomato. Pour in water and soy sauce, then season with pepper, salt, and ginger. Cover the skillet and simmer over low heat for 1 hour. Blend cornstarch into 2 tablespoons water; pour over steak mixture. Cook for 2 minutes until thick, stirring constantly. Serve over hot rice.

Yield: 4 servings

Home-Style Macaroni 'n' Cheese

1 CAN CONDENSED CHEDDAR CHEESE SOUP

½ CUP MILK

¼ TEASPOON PEPPER

1½ CUPS ELBOW MACARONI, COOKED ACCORDING TO PACKAGE DIRECTIONS

1 TABLESPOON DRY BREAD CRUMBS

2 TEASPOONS BUTTER, MELTED

Mix soup, milk, pepper, and macaroni in a 1-quart casserole dish. Stir together bread crumbs and melted butter; sprinkle over macaroni mixture. Bake at 400° for 20 minutes.

Yield: 4 servings

Chicken 'n' Pasta Skillet

1 TABLESPOON VEGETABLE OIL

1 POUND BONELESS, SKINLESS CHICKEN BREASTS, CUT INTO STRIPS

1 CAN CONDENSED CREAM OF MUSHROOM SOUP

2¼ CUPS WATER

2 CUPS FROZEN VEGETABLE COMBINATION OF YOUR CHOICE

2 CUPS CORKSCREW PASTA, UNCOOKED

GRATED PARMESAN CHEESE

Heat oil in a skillet. Add chicken; cook until browned. Remove chicken from the skillet and set aside. To the skillet, add soup, water, vegetables, and pasta. Heat until boiling, then reduce heat to medium. Cook for 10 minutes, stirring frequently. Add chicken. Cook for an additional 5 minutes. Sprinkle with Parmesan cheese.

Yield: 4 to 6 servings

Cheesy Baked Spaghetti

8 OUNCES THIN SPAGHETTI NOODLES

1 POUND GROUND BEEF

1 JAR SPAGHETTI SAUCE

½ SMALL WHITE ONION, FINELY CHOPPED

1 GREEN BELL PEPPER, CHOPPED

1 CUP MOZZARELLA CHEESE, SHREDDED

Cook spaghetti noodles according to package directions; drain. Brown ground beef; drain. Place spaghetti noodles and ground beef in buttered square baking dish. Cover with spaghetti sauce; stir in onion and green pepper. Top with cheese. Bake at 300° for 25 minutes.

Yield: 4 to 6 servings

When you're feeling overwhelmed, try these great stress busters:

1) *Take a brisk walk.*
2) *Read your Bible.*
3) *Pray.*
4) *Read a book for a quick escape to another world.*
5) *Hug your husband and your kids. (Squeeze tightly!)*
6) *Laugh. (Even better when done with a friend.)*

This is the day the LORD has made; let us rejoice and be glad in it.

PSALM 118:24

Mexican Stuffed Shells

24 JUMBO PASTA SHELLS

1 POUND GROUND BEEF

2 CUPS SALSA

1 (8 OUNCE) CAN TOMATO SAUCE

1 CUP WHOLE-KERNEL CORN, DRAINED

1 CAN REFRIED BEANS

½ CUP CHEDDAR CHEESE, SHREDDED

½ CUP SOUR CREAM

½ CUP SALSA

¼ CUP BLACK OLIVES, SLICED

¼ CUP GREEN ONIONS, SLICED

Cook pasta shells according to package directions; drain. In a large skillet, brown ground beef; drain. Stir salsa, tomato sauce, corn, and beans into the beef. Carefully spoon mixture into the cooked pasta shells. Place shells in a lightly greased 9x13-inch baking dish. Sprinkle each shell with cheese. Cover the dish with aluminum foil and bake at 350° for 25 to 30 minutes. Serve shells topped with sour cream, salsa, olives, and onions.

Yield: 6 to 8 servings

Macaroni-Sausage Bake

1 CUP ELBOW MACARONI

1 POUND BULK PORK SAUSAGE

½ CUP GREEN BELL PEPPER, CHOPPED

½ CUP RED BELL PEPPER, CHOPPED

⅛ CUP ONION, CHOPPED

½ TEASPOON DRIED OREGANO

¼ TEASPOON PEPPER

2 (8 OUNCE) CANS TOMATO SAUCE

1 CUP WATER

⅛ CUP GRATED PARMESAN CHEESE, DIVIDED

Cook macaroni according to package directions; drain and set aside. Cook sausage in a skillet over medium heat until no longer pink; drain. Add green pepper, red pepper, onion, oregano, and pepper. Stir in tomato sauce and water. Boil. Reduce heat and simmer for 5 minutes. Stir in macaroni and half of Parmesan cheese. Pour mixture into an ungreased 2-quart baking dish. Sprinkle remaining Parmesan cheese on top. Bake, uncovered, at 350° for 25 minutes or until bubbly.

Yield: 4 servings

One-Dish Lasagna

2 JARS SPAGHETTI SAUCE

1 (12 OUNCE) BOX LASAGNA NOODLES, UNCOOKED

1 POUND GROUND BEEF, UNCOOKED

¼ CUP ONION, FINELY CHOPPED

1 (8 OUNCE) CONTAINER SMALL-CURD COTTAGE CHEESE

4 CUPS MOZZARELLA CHEESE, SHREDDED

1½ CUPS HOT WATER

GRATED PARMESAN CHEESE

Cover bottom of a 9x13-inch baking dish with a third of the spaghetti sauce. Layer in the following order: half of the lasagna noodles, half of the ground beef, onion, cottage cheese, a third of the sauce, remaining noodles, half of the mozzarella cheese, remaining ground beef, remaining sauce, and remaining mozzarella cheese. Press down with spoon, then add hot water. Press mixture down with spoon again, then sprinkle with Parmesan cheese. Cover with aluminum foil and bake at 375° for 1 hour. Remove from oven and uncover; bake an additional 45 minutes. Let stand for 10 minutes before serving.

Yield: 6 to 8 servings

Bake an extra pan of lasagna and deliver it to a family in need. Sometimes the simple things mean the most.

Let no one ever come to you without leaving better and happier. Be the living expression of God's kindness: kindness in your face, kindness in your eyes, kindness in your smile.
MOTHER TERESA

Creamy Ham 'n' Broccoli Bake

1½ POUNDS FRESH BROCCOLI, COOKED UNTIL TENDER

½ CUP HAM, COOKED AND CUBED

1 CAN CONDENSED CREAM OF MUSHROOM SOUP

¼ CUP MILK

½ CUP CHEDDAR CHEESE, SHREDDED

1 CUP ALL-PURPOSE BAKING MIX

¼ CUP MARGARINE

Place broccoli and ham in a 1½-quart baking dish. Beat soup and milk until smooth; pour over broccoli and ham. Sprinkle with cheese. Combine baking mix with margarine and mix until crumbly; sprinkle over top. Bake at 400° for 20 minutes.

Yield: 4 servings

Chickenetti

8 OUNCES SPAGHETTI NOODLES, BROKEN INTO 2-INCH PIECES

3 CUPS CHICKEN, COOKED AND CUBED

¼ CUP GREEN BELL PEPPER, CHOPPED

2 CANS CONDENSED CREAM OF MUSHROOM SOUP

1 CUP CHICKEN BROTH

¼ TEASPOON SALT

¼ TEASPOON PEPPER

1 ONION, GRATED

2 CUPS PROCESSED CHEESE, GRATED AND DIVIDED

Place ingredients in a 9x13-inch baking dish, reserving 1 cup cheese to sprinkle on top of mixture. Bake at 350° for 1 hour.

Yield: 6 servings

Country-Style Scalloped Potatoes 'n' Ham

8 RED POTATOES, THINLY SLICED (SKIN ON)

1½ POUNDS HAM, CUBED

¼ CUP FLOUR

WHOLE MILK

4 TABLESPOONS BUTTER

PEPPER

Place potatoes and ham in a deep baking dish; mix well. Pour in flour and enough milk to cover mixture; stir. Place butter over top. Cover with pepper. Bake at 350° for 1½ hours or until potatoes reach desired tenderness.

Yield: 4 servings

WHILE YOU WERE OUT...

Slow-Cooker Recipes

Progress in civilization has been accompanied by progress in cookery.

FANNIE FARMER (1857–1915), American cookbook author

Spicy Beef Stew

2 POUNDS BEEF STEW MEAT

1 (11 OUNCE) CAN WHOLE-KERNEL CORN, UNDRAINED

1 (11 OUNCE) CAN CUT GREEN BEANS, UNDRAINED

1 (11 OUNCE) CAN STEWED TOMATOES, UNDRAINED

5 MEDIUM POTATOES, CUBED

1 SMALL ONION, SLICED

2 TABLESPOONS MINCED GARLIC

1 TABLESPOON CRUSHED RED PEPPER

½ TEASPOON ONION SALT

DASH HOT SAUCE

PEPPER TO TASTE

Place all ingredients in a slow cooker. Cook on medium heat for approximately 8 to 10 hours.

Yield: 4 to 6 servings

These tasty slow-cooker dishes cook up while you're away…so no need to rush home and figure out what's for dinner. I believe slow cookers were sent to us moms straight from heaven.

Ida's Hobo Stew

1 (15 OUNCE) CAN BAKED BEANS

1 (15 OUNCE) CAN BLACK BEANS, DRAINED

1 (15 OUNCE) CAN KIDNEY BEANS, DRAINED

2 POUNDS LEAN GROUND BEEF OR VENISON

1 LARGE GREEN BELL PEPPER, DICED

1 MEDIUM SWEET ONION, DICED

2 TABLESPOONS GARLIC, CHOPPED

1½ TO 2 TABLESPOONS STEAK SEASONING

2 TABLESPOONS BROWN SUGAR

1 (15 OUNCE) CAN DICED TOMATOES

Place beans in a slow cooker on high heat. In a skillet, brown ground beef; drain.
Add green pepper, onion, garlic, steak seasoning, and brown sugar; cook over
low heat until onion is transparent. Stir in tomatoes until warmed. Add meat
mixture to the beans in the slow cooker. Turn heat to low and let simmer for 2
hours.

Yield: 4 to 6 servings

BBQ Stew

2 POUNDS BEEF STEW MEAT

2½ TABLESPOONS VEGETABLE OIL

¾ CUP ONION, SLICED

½ CUP GREEN BELL PEPPER, CHOPPED

1 LARGE CLOVE GARLIC, MINCED

½ TEASPOON SALT

⅛ TEASPOON PEPPER

2 CUPS BEEF STOCK

1 (14½ OUNCE) CAN TOMATOES

⅓ CUP BARBECUE SAUCE

3 TABLESPOONS CORNSTARCH

¼ CUP COLD WATER

Heat oil in a skillet over medium heat. Brown meat lightly on all sides; remove from oil and place in a slow cooker. Sauté onion, green pepper, and garlic in the hot vegetable oil. Add to the slow cooker. Blend in salt, pepper, beef stock, tomatoes, and barbecue sauce. Cover and cook on low heat for 8 to 10 hours. Mix cornstarch with cold water and stir into stew approximately 20 minutes before done. Serve with hot cooked noodles or rice.

Yield: 6 servings

Cowboy Stew

1 POUND GROUND BEEF

¾ CUP ONION, CHOPPED

1 GREEN BELL PEPPER, CHOPPED

1 (15 OUNCE) CAN DARK RED KIDNEY BEANS

1 (15 OUNCE) CAN PORK AND BEANS

1 (15 OUNCE) CAN WHOLE-KERNEL CORN, DRAINED

2 CANS CONDENSED TOMATO SOUP

In a skillet, brown beef, onion, and green pepper; drain. Combine all ingredients in a slow cooker; cover and cook on low heat for 6 to 8 hours.

Yield: 4 servings

Beef Barley Vegetable Soup

1½ POUNDS BEEF SHANK

2 TABLESPOONS ONION, CHOPPED

½ TEASPOON GARLIC, MINCED

2 TABLESPOONS VEGETABLE OIL

1 (14 OUNCE) CAN BEEF BROTH

1½ CUPS STRONG-BREWED COFFEE

1½ CUPS WATER

1 TABLESPOON WORCESTERSHIRE SAUCE

1 BAY LEAF

1 (16 OUNCE) PACKAGE FROZEN MIXED VEGETABLES, COOKED IN ½ CUP WATER UNTIL HEATED THROUGH

1 STALK CELERY, CHOPPED

1 TABLESPOON SUGAR

2 PINTS STEWED TOMATOES

DASH THYME

2 TEASPOONS SALT

⅛ TEASPOON PEPPER

½ CUP BARLEY

1 CUP CABBAGE, CHOPPED

Brown beef, onion, and garlic in oil. Move to a slow cooker; add broth, coffee, water, Worcestershire sauce, and bay leaf. Cook covered on low heat for at least 1 hour. Remove meat and cut into small pieces. Return meat to the slow cooker; turn heat to high and add mixed vegetables, celery, sugar, tomatoes, thyme, salt, and pepper. Cover and cook for 1 to 2 hours. Add barley and cabbage in the last hour of cooking. Total cooking time for this soup is 4 hours.

Yield: 6 servings

Beef barley vegetable soup is even yummier warmed up the second day.

Split Pea Soup

1 (16 OUNCE) PACKAGE DRIED SPLIT PEAS

2 CUPS HAM, DICED

1 CUP CARROTS, DICED

1 MEDIUM ONION, CHOPPED

2 CLOVES GARLIC, MINCED

2 BAY LEAVES

½ TEASPOON SALT

½ TEASPOON PEPPER

5 CUPS BOILING WATER

MILK

Layer all ingredients except milk in a slow cooker. Cover and cook on high heat for 4 to 5 hours. Stir in milk until soup reaches desired consistency; discard bay leaves.

Yield: 4 servings

Have a dinner celebration for absolutely no reason at all. Serve a family favorite and a gooey dessert. Your loved ones will appreciate this extra special treat on an ordinary day.

Easy Veggie Soup

1 FAMILY-SIZED PACKAGE BEEF STEW MEAT

2 JARS PLAIN SPAGHETTI SAUCE

WATER

POTATOES

CELERY

CORN

PEAS

CARROTS

OTHER VEGETABLES IF DESIRED

Cook meat in a slow cooker, shred meat, then prepare soup. Empty spaghetti sauce into a large stockpot. Fill empty jars with water and add to sauce. Add vegetables as desired. Heat over medium heat, then return to slow cooker on low for 3 to 4 hours or until vegetables are tender.

Yield: 6 servings

When you find yourself with a skim of grease on the top of your soup or broth, place an ice cube on a slotted spoon and skim it over the grease. The grease will harden and stick to the spoon and ice.

Slow 'n' Savory Fish Chowder

1 POUND WHITE FISH (USE ANY ONE OR COMBINATION OF COD, FLOUNDER, HADDOCK, HALIBUT, OCEAN PERCH, PIKE, OR RAINBOW TROUT)

1 TEASPOON DRIED ROSEMARY

1 (14 OUNCE) CAN DICED TOMATOES

½ CUP CHICKEN BROTH

1 TEASPOON SALT

½ CUP ONION, CHOPPED

½ CUP CELERY, CHOPPED

½ CUP CARROT, CHOPPED

¼ CUP FRESH PARSLEY, SNIPPED (OR 1 TABLESPOON PARSLEY FLAKES)

1 CUP CLAM JUICE

2 TABLESPOONS BUTTER (NO SUBSTITUTES), MELTED

3 TABLESPOONS FLOUR

⅓ CUP HALF-AND-HALF

Cut cleaned fish into small chunks. Combine all ingredients except butter, flour, and half-and-half in a 2-quart slow cooker; stir well. Cover and cook on low heat for 7 to 8 hours (or on high heat for 3 to 4 hours.) One hour before serving, combine butter, flour, and half-and-half and stir into fish mixture. Continue to cook for 1 hour as mixture thickens slightly.

Yield: 4 to 6 servings (approximately 2 quarts)

This chowder is also delicious served over cooked rice. As a matter of fact, many thick soup recipes are mighty tasty on a bed of rice. My preferred way to eat chili is over white rice and topped with cheese. Yum!

Delicious Slow-Cooked Beef Sandwiches

2 POUNDS BEEF STEW MEAT

1 CAN CONDENSED CREAM OF CELERY SOUP

1 CAN CONDENSED CREAM OF MUSHROOM SOUP

½ ENVELOPE DRY ONION SOUP MIX

BUNS OR BREAD

Rinse stew meat and place in a slow cooker. Add remaining ingredients; stir.

Turn heat to low and let cook overnight. Beef will become shredded as it cooks.

Enjoy on buns or other bread of your choice.

Yield: 6 to 8 servings

Best Barbecue Bites

1 SMALL JAR BARBECUE SAUCE

1 SMALL JAR GRAPE JELLY

2 POUNDS SMOKED SAUSAGE CHUNKS OR MEATBALLS

Combine barbecue sauce and jelly. Place meat in a slow cooker and pour sauce over all. Cook on medium heat, stirring occasionally, until meat is heated through.

Yield: 6 to 8 servings

Hot Italian Sausage Sandwiches

6 HOT ITALIAN SAUSAGE LINKS

1 JAR THREE-CHEESE SPAGHETTI SAUCE

1 (6 COUNT) PACKAGE SAUSAGE ROLLS

Place sausage links in a slow cooker; cover completely with spaghetti sauce.

Cook on low heat for approximately 8 hours. Serve on sausage rolls with

additional spaghetti sauce if desired.

Yield: 6 servings

Easy Country-Style BBQ Ribs

8 BONELESS BEEF RIBS

2 (18 OUNCE) JARS MESQUITE-FLAVORED BARBECUE SAUCE

Place ribs in a single layer in a slow cooker; cover completely with barbecue

sauce. Cook on medium heat for 8 to 10 hours.

Yield: 2 servings

*Make a list of all the things for which you're thankful.
Write it on pretty stationery and display it on the
refrigerator where you'll see it often—a daily
reminder of everything that's good in your life.*

Pork Ribs 'n' Kraut

8 PORK SPARERIBS

SEASONED SALT TO TASTE

1 LARGE CAN SAUERKRAUT

Brown pork spareribs in a frying pan over medium heat; season and place in a
slow cooker. Add sauerkraut. Set heat on low and cook for 6 to 8 hours.

Yield: 2 servings

Pot Roast with Carrots

1 CAN CONDENSED CREAM OF MUSHROOM SOUP

1 ENVELOPE DRY ONION SOUP MIX

1 SMALL PACKAGE BABY CARROTS

1 (4 POUND) BONELESS CHUCK POT ROAST

Mix soup, onion soup mix, and carrots in a slow cooker. Add roast; turn to coat.

Cover. Cook on low heat for approximately 8 hours.

Yield: 8 servings

Place some fresh-cut flowers in a beautiful glass vase on your tabletop. This is an easy way to bring pure and simple delight to your dining room.

Slow-Cooker Burritos

1 POUND GROUND BEEF OR GROUND PORK

2 TABLESPOONS ONION, CHOPPED

1 CAN DICED AND SPICED TOMATOES

1 CAN REFRIED BEANS

1 (12 OUNCE) BAG CORN TORTILLA CHIPS

1½ CUPS CHEESE, SHREDDED

In a skillet, cook meat and onion; drain. In a bowl, combine tomatoes and beans; blend well. Spray the inside of a large slow cooker with oil. Divide ingredients in thirds and start layering. Cover the bottom of the slow cooker with chips, cover with a third of the meat, spread on a third of the beans, and sprinkle with a third of the cheese. Repeat layers, ending with cheese on top. Cover and cook on low heat for 4 hours or on high heat for 2 hours.

Yield: 4 to 6 servings

Sour Cream 'n' Bean Chicken

4 BONELESS, SKINLESS CHICKEN BREASTS, FROZEN

1 (15½ OUNCE) CAN BLACK BEANS, DRAINED

1 (15 OUNCE) JAR SALSA

1 (8 OUNCE) PACKAGE CREAM CHEESE

Place frozen chicken breasts in slow cooker. Add black beans and salsa. Cook on high heat for approximately 5 hours. Toss block of cream cheese on top and let stand for 30 minutes.

Yield: 4 servings

Bacon Chicken

8 SLICES BACON

4 BONELESS, SKINLESS CHICKEN BREASTS

1 CAN CONDENSED CREAM OF MUSHROOM SOUP

¾ CUP SOUR CREAM

¼ CUP FLOUR

Wrap two bacon slices around each chicken breast and place in a slow cooker. In a medium bowl, combine condensed soup, sour cream, and flour; mix thoroughly. Pour over chicken. Cover and cook on low heat for 7 to 8 hours.

Yield: 4 servings

Creamy Mushroom Pork Chops

3 POTATOES, PEELED AND SLICED

4 PORK CHOPS

2 CANS CONDENSED CREAM OF MUSHROOM SOUP

SALT AND PEPPER TO TASTE

Slice potatoes and place in the bottom of a slow cooker. Season pork chops and place them on top of the potatoes. Cover the chops with mushroom soup and cook on low for 8 hours.

Yield: 4 servings

Slow 'n' Easy Spaghetti

1 POUND LEAN GROUND BEEF

1 TEASPOON ITALIAN SEASONING

2 CLOVES GARLIC, MINCED

½ CUP ONION, CHOPPED

2 CUPS PLAIN SPAGHETTI SAUCE

1 (4 OUNCE) CAN SLICED MUSHROOMS, DRAINED

1 QUART TOMATO JUICE

**8 OUNCES SPAGHETTI NOODLES, UNCOOKED AND
BROKEN INTO 3- TO 4-INCH PIECES**

Brown ground beef in a skillet with Italian seasoning and garlic; drain and place in a large slow cooker. Add remaining ingredients except noodles; stir well. Cover and cook on low heat for 6 to 7 hours or on high heat for 3 to 4 hours. For the last hour of cooking, turn heat to high and stir in uncooked noodles.

Yield: 6 servings

Slow-Cooker Mac 'n' Cheese

1 (16 OUNCE) BOX ELBOW MACARONI

1 TABLESPOON VEGETABLE OIL

1 (13 OUNCE) CAN EVAPORATED MILK

1½ CUPS MILK

4½ CUPS CHEDDAR CHEESE, SHREDDED AND DIVIDED

½ CUP MELTED BUTTER

Cook macaroni according to package directions; drain. Grease the bottom and sides of a slow cooker. Place hot macaroni and vegetable oil in the slow cooker; add remaining ingredients, reserving ½ cup cheese. Stir gently to combine. Cover and cook on low heat for 3 to 4 hours, stirring occasionally. Just before serving, sprinkle with remaining cheese.

Yield: 6 servings

Cheesy Egg 'n' Mushroom Meal

8 EGGS

¾ CUP MILK

8 OUNCES CHEDDAR CHEESE, SHREDDED

½ CUP ONION, CHOPPED

1 CUP FRESH MUSHROOMS, THINLY SLICED

SALT AND PEPPER TO TASTE

Beat eggs. Add milk and mix well. Pour mixture into a greased slow cooker. Add cheese, onion, mushrooms, salt, and pepper. Cook on high heat for 1½ to 2 hours.

Yield: 4 to 6 servings

I've done it again, Lord. I burned my family's supper. Somewhere between helping the kids with homework and doing a quick cleanup around the house, I forgot about the meal on the stove. Martha seems so perfect, while I often feel like a failure. Please remind me (daily!) that it's okay to be me. My family and friends love me just as I am. And so do You, Lord. Thank You for loving each one of us in spite of our human imperfections. Amen.

Chicken Fajitas

1 POUND BONELESS, SKINLESS CHICKEN BREASTS, CUT INTO STRIPS

1 CAN DICED TOMATOES

1 CAN DICED GREEN CHILIES

1 SMALL ONION, CHOPPED

2 GREEN BELL PEPPERS, SLICED

1 ENVELOPE FAJITA SEASONING

Layer ingredients in a large slow cooker. Cook on high heat until juices boil.

Set heat on low for 4 hours until chicken is tender. Serve over cooked rice or in

tortilla shells.

Yield: 4 servings

Turkey Rueben Pot

9 OUNCES DELI SMOKED TURKEY, SLICED AND CHOPPED

3 OUNCES CREAM CHEESE, CHUNKED

2 CUPS SWISS CHEESE, SHREDDED

8 OUNCES SAUERKRAUT, DRAINED AND RINSED

½ CUP THOUSAND ISLAND DRESSING

Mix all ingredients in a slow cooker. Cook on low heat for 2 hours. Serve on crackers or rye bread.

Yield: 6 servings

Crock-Pot Western Omelet

1 (32 OUNCE) BAG HASH BROWNS, FROZEN

1 POUND SAUSAGE, COOKED AND DRAINED WELL

1 SMALL ONION, DICED

1 MEDIUM GREEN BELL PEPPER, CHOPPED

1½ CUPS CHEDDAR CHEESE, SHREDDED

12 EGGS

1 CUP MILK

1 TEASPOON SALT

1 TEASPOON BLACK PEPPER

Lightly spray the inside of a slow cooker with oil. Cover the bottom of the slow cooker with a layer of frozen hash browns, followed by layers of sausage, onion, green pepper, and cheese. Repeat the layering process two or three times, ending with a layer of cheese. Beat together the eggs, milk, salt, and pepper. Pour egg mixture over the top layer of cheese. Cover and cook on low heat for 10 to 12 hours.

Yield: 6 to 8 servings

EASY, BREEZY ADDITIONS

Salads, Soups & Sides

Simplicity is the ultimate sophistication.

LEONARDO DA VINCI (1452–1519), Italian Renaissance artist

Cucumbers with Cream Dressing

1 CUP MAYONNAISE (NO SUBSTITUTES)

¼ CUP SUGAR

¼ CUP VINEGAR

¼ TEASPOON SALT

4 CUPS CUCUMBERS, SLICED

Blend mayonnaise, sugar, vinegar, and salt. Add cucumbers and toss. Cover and refrigerate for at least 2 hours.

Yield: 6 to 8 servings

Spaghetti Slaw

1 (16 OUNCE) PACKAGE ANGEL HAIR PASTA

1 SMALL ONION, CHOPPED

1 SMALL GREEN BELL PEPPER, CHOPPED

1 BAG COLESLAW MIX

2 CUPS PREPARED COLESLAW DRESSING

Cook pasta according to package directions; drain, rinse in cold water, and drain completely. Place in a large serving bowl and add onion, green pepper, and coleslaw mix. Stir in the dressing. Refrigerate for 2 hours before serving.

Yield: 8 to 10 servings

Waldorf Salad

3 APPLES, CUT INTO MEDIUM CHUNKS

1 STALK CELERY, CHOPPED

4 TO 5 DATES, CHOPPED

¼ CUP WALNUTS, CHOPPED

½ CUP MINI MARSHMALLOWS

⅔ CUP MAYONNAISE OR SALAD DRESSING

1 TABLESPOON SUGAR

1 TABLESPOON LEMON JUICE

In a large bowl, combine apples, celery, dates, walnuts, and marshmallows. In a separate bowl, blend mayonnaise, sugar, and lemon juice; spread over apple mixture, coating well.

Yield: 4 servings

Keep your cutting board from sliding around the countertop when you apply pressure by cutting a piece of non-skid shelf liner to fit under the board.

Layered Lettuce Salad

1 HEAD LETTUCE, TORN INTO SMALL PIECES

½ CUP CELERY, CHOPPED

½ CUP GREEN BELL PEPPER, CHOPPED

1 CAN SLICED WATER CHESTNUTS

½ CUP ONION, CHOPPED

1 (10 OUNCE) PACKAGE FROZEN PEAS, THAWED

2 CUPS MAYONNAISE OR SALAD DRESSING

2 TABLESPOONS SUGAR

1½ CUPS CHEDDAR CHEESE, SHREDDED

In a 10x15-inch dish, layer lettuce, celery, green pepper, water chestnuts, onion, and peas in the order given. Spread with mayonnaise, then sprinkle with sugar and top with cheddar cheese. Cover with plastic wrap and refrigerate for one day. Serve at room temperature.

Yield: 8 to 10 servings

Alfredo Pasta Salad

8 OUNCES ROTINI (CORKSCREW-SHAPED PASTA)

1 CUP RED BELL PEPPER, CHOPPED

1 CUP FROZEN PEAS, SLIGHTLY THAWED

¼ CUP ONION, CHOPPED

4 TO 5 HARD COOKED EGGS, PEELED AND CHOPPED

DRESSING:

1 CUP PLAIN NONFAT YOGURT

1 CUP MAYONNAISE

⅓ CUP GRATED PARMESAN CHEESE

1 TEASPOON DRIED BASIL

2 TEASPOONS GARLIC SALT

⅛ TEASPOON WHITE PEPPER

Cook rotini for 10 to 12 minutes until done; drain and rinse with cool water. While the rotini is cooking, blend dressing ingredients in a small bowl. In a large bowl, gently combine rotini, red pepper, peas, and onion. Stir the dressing into the pasta. Gently fold the eggs into the salad. Cover and refrigerate until ready to serve.

Yield: 8 servings

Make the conscious choice to be joyful. You'll be delighted at what a change this simple but powerful choice will make in your life!

Heavenly Broccoli Salad

½ CUP CELERY, FINELY CHOPPED

½ CUP RAISINS, RINSED AND DRAINED

½ JAR BACON BITS

⅓ CUP UNSALTED SUNFLOWER SEEDS

1 BUNCH BROCCOLI CUT INTO SMALL FLORETS

1 SMALL RED ONION, FINELY CHOPPED

½ CUP SEEDLESS RED GRAPES, HALVED

DRESSING:

½ CUP MAYONNAISE

¼ CUP SUGAR

1 TABLESPOON CIDER VINEGAR

In a large bowl, combine celery, raisins, bacon bits, sunflower seeds, broccoli, onion, and grapes; mix thoroughly. Blend dressing ingredients in a separate bowl; pour over salad. Cover and refrigerate until ready to serve.

Yield: 4 to 6 servings

After you've cleaned up the kitchen and everything is back in order (or even if it's not!), take a walk through the neighborhood with your family. Or if the weather isn't cooperating, stay indoors and play a board game. Savor this extra-special time together.

Be faithful in little things, for in them our strength lies.
MOTHER TERESA

Taco Salad

1 POUND GROUND BEEF

1 ENVELOPE TACO SEASONING

1 LARGE OR 2 SMALL HEADS LETTUCE, SHREDDED

1 CAN KIDNEY BEANS, DRAINED AND RINSED

2 CUPS CHEDDAR CHEESE, SHREDDED

1 TO 2 LARGE TOMATOES, CHOPPED (OPTIONAL)

1 CUP SLICED BLACK OLIVES (OPTIONAL)

1 LARGE BOTTLE SPICY FRENCH DRESSING

1 SMALL BAG TORTILLA CHIPS

Brown ground beef; drain. Add taco seasoning with water as called for on the package and cook until thickened. Cool. Place meat with lettuce, kidney beans, cheese, tomatoes, and olives in a large bowl. Coat with dressing. Just before serving, crumble chips on top and toss into salad.

Yield: 6 to 8 servings

Grated Potato Salad

6 CUPS POTATOES, PEELED, COOKED, AND GRATED

6 HARD-BOILED EGGS, PEELED AND CHOPPED

1 CUP MAYONNAISE

¾ CUP SUGAR

¼ CUP MILK

2 TABLESPOONS CIDER VINEGAR

2 TEASPOONS SALT

1½ TEASPOONS MUSTARD

In a large bowl, combine potatoes and eggs. In a separate bowl, whisk remaining

ingredients; pour over potato and egg mixture. Stir until mixed thoroughly.

Cover and refrigerate for 4 hours before serving.

Yield: 10 servings

Roasted Ranch Potato Salad

4 CUPS SMALL RED POTATOES, UNPEELED AND CUT INTO 1-INCH CHUNKS

½ TEASPOON GARLIC POWDER

¼ TEASPOON SALT

⅛ TEASPOON PEPPER

½ CUP RANCH DRESSING

3 TO 4 SLICES BACON, COOKED CRISP AND CRUMBLED

2 HARD-BOILED EGGS, PEELED AND CHOPPED

2 TABLESPOONS GREEN ONION, SLICED

Spray a baking sheet with cooking oil. Spread out potato chunks in a single layer. Sprinkle with garlic powder, salt, and pepper. Spray with more oil. Bake at 425° for 30 to 35 minutes or until potatoes are tender and golden brown. Stir potatoes halfway through baking. Blend dressing, bacon, egg, and onion in a large bowl. Add potatoes; mix lightly. Enjoy warm or chilled.

Yield: 5 servings

Hawaiian Fruit Salad

¼ **CUP MAYONNAISE**

1 **TABLESPOON SUGAR**

½ **TEASPOON LEMON JUICE**

¼ **TEASPOON SALT**

½ **CUP WHIPPING CREAM**

1 **LARGE RED APPLE, CHOPPED**

1 **LARGE YELLOW APPLE, CHOPPED**

1 **LARGE BANANA, SLICED**

½ **CUP WALNUTS, CHOPPED**

LETTUCE

½ **CUP FLAKED COCONUT, TOASTED**

In a large bowl, blend mayonnaise, sugar, lemon juice, and salt; set aside. In a separate bowl, whip cream to form soft peaks; fold into mayonnaise mixture. Gently stir in apples, banana, and walnuts; chill. Line a bowl with lettuce; add chilled fruit. Garnish with toasted flaked coconut.

Yield: 6 servings

Ever noticed how a cold lemon doesn't like to give up its juice? I microwave a lemon 10 to 20 seconds before I try to squeeze it.

Corn Casserole

1 CAN WHOLE-KERNEL CORN

1 CAN CREAM-STYLE CORN

1 (8 OUNCE) CONTAINER SOUR CREAM

1 EGG, BEATEN

3 TABLESPOONS ONION, CHOPPED

1 SMALL BOX CORN MUFFIN MIX

½ STICK MARGARINE

⅓ TEASPOON PARSLEY

½ TEASPOON SALT

½ TEASPOON PEPPER

Combine all ingredients in a greased 2½-quart casserole dish. Bake at 350° for 45 minutes.

Yield: 8 to 10 servings

"Disconnect" from the world. Turn off your cell phone, let the answering machine take care of your home phone calls, turn off the TV, and savor the silence. A little peace and quiet will rejuvenate your soul.

A heart at peace gives life to the body.
PROVERBS 14:30

Harvard Beets

1 CAN BEETS, DICED

1 TEASPOON BUTTER

1 TABLESPOON SUGAR

1 TABLESPOON VINEGAR

2 TEASPOONS CORNSTARCH

Place beets in a saucepan and cover with enough liquid from the can to nearly cover the beets. Heat through and add butter. Blend sugar, vinegar, and cornstarch; add to the beets and liquid. Stir rapidly over medium heat until thickened. If mixture is too thick, add a few drops of water.

Yield: 4 servings

Classic Green Bean Bake

1 CAN CONDENSED CREAM OF MUSHROOM SOUP

½ CUP MILK

1 TEASPOON SOY SAUCE

DASH PEPPER

**4 CUPS FRESH GREEN BEANS, COOKED
(OR 2 CANS CUT GREEN BEANS, DRAINED)**

1 (2.8 OUNCE) CAN FRENCH-FRIED ONIONS

Combine soup, milk, soy sauce, and pepper in a 1½-quart casserole dish. Stir in beans and half of onions. Bake at 350° for 25 minutes or until heated through. Remove from oven and stir; top with remaining onions. Bake for an additional 5 minutes.

Yield: 6 servings

Fresh Green Beans

2 SLICES BACON, CUT INTO SMALL PIECES

½ SMALL ONION, CHOPPED

1 POUND FRESH GREEN BEANS

1 TEASPOON SALT

DASH PEPPER

Brown bacon in a large saucepan. Remove bacon from pan. Sauté onion in bacon grease; drain, leaving a little bacon grease in the pan. Add beans, bacon, salt, and pepper. Add just enough water to cover the bottom of the pan. Bring to a rolling boil; reduce heat to simmer. Let simmer for approximately 1 hour.

Yield: 8 servings

Baked Sweet Potatoes

Select one potato per person; scrub, remove spots, and prick skin with a fork. Wrap potato in aluminum foil. Bake at 350° for 1 hour (longer if potato is very large). Test with a sharp knife to see if potato is soft.

Microwave directions: Prepare as above, but wrap each potato in a paper towel instead of foil. Microwave on HIGH 4 minutes for one; add 2 minutes for each additional potato. (The larger the potato, the longer it needs to bake.)

Yield: 1 potato per person

Baked sweet potatoes are a nice diversion from the average. Their sweetness is enticing to picky eaters. Serve topped with your choice of butter, cinnamon, brown sugar, mini marshmallows, and pecans. Kids will enjoy piling on the flavors.

Sweet Potato Casserole

2 CUPS SWEET POTATOES, MASHED (1 LARGE CAN, DRAINED)

½ TEASPOON SALT

3 TABLESPOONS BUTTER

½ CUP MILK

1 CUP SUGAR

2 EGGS, BEATEN

1 TEASPOON VANILLA

TOPPING:

1 CUP BROWN SUGAR

⅓ CUP FLOUR

½ CUP BUTTER, MELTED

1 CUP PECANS, CHOPPED

Mix the first seven ingredients and place in a greased 8x8-inch baking dish.

Combine topping ingredients and spread over sweet potato mixture. Bake at

350° for 35 minutes.

Yield: 4 servings

To easily measure small amounts of liquid, use a medicine dropper with measurements marked on the sides.

Make-Ahead Mashed Potato Casserole

12 LARGE POTATOES, PEELED, COOKED, AND DRAINED

1 (8 OUNCE) CONTAINER SOUR CREAM

1 (8 OUNCE) PACKAGE CREAM CHEESE

1 TEASPOON ONION POWDER

¼ CUP BUTTER, MELTED

SALT AND PEPPER TO TASTE

Combine all ingredients except butter, salt, and pepper. Mash until fluffy (add milk if too stiff). Spread in a buttered 9x13-inch baking dish; top with melted butter and salt and pepper. Bake at 350° for 1 hour.

Yield: 10 servings

This dish can be prepared ahead of time and then stored in the freezer until you're ready to bake it.

Roasted Veggie Medley

1 POUND SMALL RED POTATOES, UNPEELED AND CUT INTO 1-INCH CHUNKS

3 TABLESPOONS OLIVE OIL, DIVIDED

2 GARLIC CLOVES, CHOPPED

2 TEASPOONS DRIED THYME

2 TEASPOONS DRIED ROSEMARY

1 TEASPOON SALT

½ TEASPOON PEPPER

1 MEDIUM ZUCCHINI, CHUNKED

6 TO 8 PODS OKRA, CUT INTO ¾-INCH SLICES

1 SMALL SWEET ONION, CHUNKED

1 SMALL RED BELL PEPPER, CHUNKED

Place cut potatoes in a large plastic bag. Add 2 tablespoons olive oil, garlic, thyme, rosemary, salt, and pepper; toss to coat. Spread out potato chunks in a single layer on a baking sheet and bake at 425° for 20 minutes. In the same bag in which you tossed the potatoes, place the zucchini, okra, onion, pepper, and remaining tablespoon of olive oil. Toss. Stir veggies into potatoes on the baking sheet and return to oven for 15 to 20 minutes, until potatoes are golden brown and all veggies are tender.

Yield: 6 servings

I live in an area where the grocery stores don't offer many fresh herbs beyond parsley. Dried herbs work well, though, in most all recipes. Just remember, if a recipe calls for a fresh herb, 1 tablespoon of fresh equals only 1 teaspoon of dried. Still, when I want that fresh herb look, I toss in some chopped parsley, adding color and texture without disturbing the balance of taste.

Grilled Hobo Potatoes

6 LARGE RED POTATOES, CHOPPED

1 LARGE GREEN BELL PEPPER, FINELY CHOPPED

1 LARGE RED BELL PEPPER, FINELY CHOPPED

1 SMALL WHITE ONION, CHOPPED

4 TABLESPOONS BUTTER, DIVIDED

SALT AND PEPPER TO TASTE

Divide potatoes and vegetables into 4 even portions on top of 4 sheets of aluminum foil. Top each portion with 1 tablespoon butter. Season with salt and pepper as desired. Wrap foil tightly, being sure to cover potatoes completely. Place on a hot grill (or in the coals at the outer edges of a campfire). Cook for 30 minutes or until potatoes are tender. Be careful about turning or moving the foil pouches, as hot juices will escape.

Yield: 4 servings

Homemade Applesauce

4 TO 5 LARGE APPLES, PEELED AND SLICED

½ CUP WATER

¼ CUP SUGAR

Place apples and water in a medium saucepan; cover and bring to a boil. Turn heat to low, stirring occasionally to keep from sticking. When apples are soft, remove from heat and add sugar. To make a chunky sauce, don't overcook. (If there is a lot of water on the apples, carefully pour most of it off before adding the sugar.) To make a smooth sauce, run apple mixture through a colander. Yield: 4 to 6 servings

Pasta Salad

1 (16 OUNCE) PACKAGE THIN SPAGHETTI NOODLES

2 LARGE TOMATOES, CHOPPED

1 MEDIUM ONION, CHOPPED

1 CUCUMBER, CHOPPED

1 GREEN BELL PEPPER, CHOPPED

1 (16 OUNCE) BOTTLE ITALIAN DRESSING

1 ENVELOPE DRY ITALIAN DRESSING MIX

Cook noodles according to package directions; rinse in cold water, drain, and set aside. Combine vegetables, Italian dressing, and Italian dressing mix. Add to cooled noodles. Cover and refrigerate overnight.

Yield: 8 to 10 servings

If you're overextended, learn to say no! You'll be a happier person for it...and you'll find that you enjoy having the freedom to do something that isn't an obligation.

Broccoli 'n' Rice

2 (10 OUNCE) PACKAGES FROZEN CHOPPED BROCCOLI

2 CUPS RICE, COOKED

1 TEASPOON CELERY SALT

3 CUPS PROCESSED CHEESE, CUBED

Cook broccoli according to package directions. Drain completely. Add hot rice and celery salt. Stir in cheese until melted. Serve warm.

Yield: 6 to 8 servings

Spanish Rice (Wanda's Style)

½ **POUND GROUND BEEF**

1 **SMALL ONION, CHOPPED**

½ **MEDIUM GREEN BELL PEPPER, CHOPPED**

2 **CUPS TOMATO JUICE**

1 **CUP RICE, UNCOOKED**

1 **TEASPOON CHILI POWDER**

1 **TEASPOON SALT**

½ **TEASPOON PEPPER**

In a large skillet, brown ground beef with onion and green pepper; drain. Add tomato juice, rice, chili powder, salt, and pepper. Bring to a boil; cover the skillet and turn heat to low. Let cook for 20 minutes, stirring occasionally to keep from sticking. It is done when the rice is tender.

Yield: 4 servings

Creamy Noodles

1 (12 OUNCE) PACKAGE EGG NOODLES

⅓ CUP BUTTER, SOFTENED

½ CUP EVAPORATED MILK

¼ CUP GRATED PARMESAN CHEESE

2¼ TEASPOONS DRY ITALIAN DRESSING MIX

Cook noodles according to package directions; drain. Toss noodles and butter together in a bowl. Add remaining ingredients and mix thoroughly. Serve immediately.

Yield: 6 servings

Mexican Chicken Soup

**2 TO 3 BONELESS, SKINLESS CHICKEN BREASTS,
COOKED AND CUT INTO CHUNKS**

2 CANS CHICKEN BROTH

1 TABLESPOON CUMIN

1 TEASPOON CHICKEN BOUILLON

1 LARGE JAR WHITE NORTHERN BEANS

1 JAR SALSA

2 CUPS CHEDDAR CHEESE, SHREDDED

In a large stockpot, combine all ingredients and heat through. Serve with tortilla or corn chips, additional shredded cheese, and sour cream.

Yield: 4 to 6 servings

Cut down the number of times you have to run to the store by stocking up a six-month supply of all nonperishable items. You'll be amazed at how much time you'll save yourself.

Vegetable Soup

Small beef roast or 1 pound beef stew meat

2 cups water

1 quart diced tomatoes with juice

Vegetables (your choice of potatoes, onion, carrots, peas, celery, green beans, corn, baby lima beans, okra, small turnip, or shredded cabbage)

2 teaspoons salt

½ teaspoon pepper

1 teaspoon chili powder

1 teaspoon fresh garlic

½ teaspoon cumin

Brown meat in a large stockpot; add water and cook meat until nearly tender. Chop and add vegetables as desired. Add seasonings. Let soup simmer at least 1 hour, adding more water if needed.

Yield: 4 to 6 servings

Beefy Pasta 'n' Salsa Soup

1 POUND GROUND BEEF, COOKED AND DRAINED

2 CANS BEEF BROTH

1 CAN DICED TOMATOES WITH JUICE

1½ CUPS MEDIUM SALSA

1 CUP SMALL SHELL PASTA, UNCOOKED

½ CUP ONION, CHOPPED

2 CLOVES GARLIC, CHOPPED

2 TEASPOONS CHILI POWDER

¼ CUP CHEDDAR CHEESE, SHREDDED

Combine all ingredients except cheese in a medium saucepan; bring to a boil.
Reduce heat to low; cook for 15 minutes or until pasta is tender. Garnish with
cheese.

Yield: 8 servings

Clam Chowder

2 TABLESPOONS BUTTER

¼ CUP CELERY, CHOPPED

2 TABLESPOONS ONION, CHOPPED

1 CUP POTATOES, CUBED

1 CUP MILK

2 CUPS MINCED CLAMS WITH JUICE

In a large saucepan, sauté celery and onion in butter until brown. Add potatoes and cook until tender. Add milk and clams; heat thoroughly.

Yield: 4 servings

Remember the old saying "Soup boiled is soup spoiled."
Always cook your soups gently and evenly.

Cream of Broccoli Soup

1 (10 OUNCE) PACKAGE FROZEN CHOPPED BROCCOLI

ONION OR ONION POWDER TO TASTE

1 CAN CHICKEN BROTH

1 CAN CONDENSED CREAM OF CELERY SOUP

1 CAN CONDENSED CREAM OF MUSHROOM SOUP

1 TO 1½ CUPS CHEDDAR CHEESE, SHREDDED

Cook broccoli and onion in chicken broth. Combine soups and stir into broccoli mixture. Bring to a gentle boil, stirring constantly. Add cheese, stirring until melted. Serve hot.

Yield: 6 servings

Old-Fashioned Potato Soup

8 MEDIUM POTATOES, PEELED AND CUBED

1 QUART MILK

2 TEASPOONS SALT

⅓ TEASPOON PEPPER

1 TABLESPOON BUTTER

½ CUP FLOUR

1 EGG, BEATEN

2 TO 3 TABLESPOONS MILK

In a large saucepan, boil potatoes in salted water until tender; drain. Add 1 quart milk to potatoes and warm over medium heat, then add salt and pepper; stir. Cut butter into flour; mix in egg and just enough milk to make mixture thin enough to drop into hot soup. Drop large spoonfuls of flour mixture into soup; cover and cook over low heat for 10 minutes, stirring occasionally to prevent scorching.

Yield: 8 servings

Broccoli Noodle Soup

6 CUPS WATER

6 CHICKEN BOUILLON CUBES

1 (8 OUNCE) PACKAGE FINE NOODLES

2 (10 OUNCE) PACKAGES FROZEN CHOPPED BROCCOLI

1 POUND PROCESSED CHEESE, CUBED

6 CUPS MILK

SALT AND PEPPER TO TASTE

In a large saucepan, bring water to a boil. Add bouillon cubes and noodles; cook for 4 minutes. Add broccoli; reduce heat and simmer until broccoli is tender. Reduce heat to low; add cheese, milk, and salt and pepper. Cook, stirring constantly, until cheese is melted.

Yield: 8 to 10 servings

Spend some time after dinner doing absolutely nothing with your family. Yes, nothing! You'll be delighted at how much you enjoy each other's company.

Chili

1 POUND LEAN GROUND BEEF (OR GROUND VENISON)

1 SMALL ONION, CHOPPED

1 SMALL GREEN BELL PEPPER, CHOPPED

1 CAN DARK RED KIDNEY BEANS

1 (7 OUNCE) CAN TOMATO SAUCE

2 CUPS TOMATO JUICE

2 TABLESPOONS CHILI POWDER

½ TEASPOON GARLIC

2 TEASPOONS SALT

½ TEASPOON PEPPER

½ TEASPOON CUMIN

In a large saucepan, brown meat with onion and green pepper; drain. Add beans, tomato sauce and juice, and seasonings. Let simmer for 30 to 40 minutes on low heat. Stir to keep from sticking. Good served with corn chips or crackers.

Yield: 6 servings

My mother would cook a handful of elbow macaroni until tender and add it to the chili if it had a lot of liquid. Macaroni tends to thicken the chili and make it go farther and be more filling.

Wheat Chili

3 CUPS WATER

1 CUP HARD SPRING WHEAT BERRIES

2 TABLESPOONS CANOLA OIL

1 MEDIUM ONION, CHOPPED

2 CLOVES GARLIC, MINCED

**1 POUND LEAN GROUND BEEF
OR VENISON**

**1 (10 OUNCE) CAN DICED TOMATOES
WITH CHILIES**

4 CUPS TOMATO SAUCE

**2 CUPS BEEF BROTH (OR USE
WATER OR BEER)**

1 TEASPOON CHILI POWDER

1 TEASPOON CUMIN

1 TEASPOON OREGANO

1 TEASPOON SALT

In a saucepan, bring 3 cups of water just to the boiling point, then add wheat and simmer, uncovered, for 2 hours. Make sure the water doesn't boil away, and add more if needed. In a skillet, heat oil and sauté onion until transparent. Stir in garlic, then add the meat, breaking apart and stirring until well cooked. Drain grease. In a large saucepan, combine tomatoes, tomato sauce, broth, and seasonings. Stir in wheat and meat. Simmer over low heat for 1 hour.

Yield: 6 servings

The wheat hydration process also can be done in a slow cooker for 8 hours on low and covered. If water remains, add the liquid to the chili in place of some of the broth. The hard spring wheat berries will be soft inside but still have a chewy hull on the outside and be full of protein. Wheat is the prairie farmer's bean (less gas). But beans also can be added to this recipe.

Cheeseburger Chowder

1 POUND GROUND BEEF

½ CUP ONION, DICED

½ CUP CELERY, DICED

½ CUP BUTTER

½ CUP FLOUR

½ GALLON MILK

1½ POUNDS PROCESSED CHEESE, CUBED

½ BAG FROZEN HASH BROWN CUBES

In a large stockpot, brown ground beef with onion and celery. Rinse in cool water to remove grease. Return to pot; add butter and heat until butter melts. Stir flour into the meat mixture to coat. Gradually add milk, cooking over medium heat. When mixture is hot—not boiling—and starting to thicken, add cheese. Stir until melted. Add hash browns. When soup is hot to your taste, it is ready to serve.

Yield: 4 to 6 servings

Remove the odor of onion from your hands by rubbing them with a paste of salt and vinegar.

Pull-Apart Garlic Bread

3 TABLESPOONS BUTTER, DIVIDED

2 (10 COUNT) TUBES REFRIGERATED BISCUITS

2 CLOVES GARLIC, MINCED

2 TO 3 TABLESPOONS GRATED PARMESAN AND/OR ROMANO CHEESE

In a 350° oven, melt 1 tablespoon butter in a loaf pan. Place both logs of biscuit dough in the pan, one log on each side. Fan the biscuits apart. Melt 2 tablespoons butter and blend with garlic; drizzle over and between biscuits. Sprinkle cheese over and between biscuits. Bake at 350° for 30 minutes or until middle tests done. Serve warm.

Yield: 10 servings

Beer Bread

3 CUPS SELF-RISING FLOUR

½ CUP SUGAR

2 TABLESPOONS BUTTER, MELTED

1 CAN BEER

In a large mixing bowl, blend ingredients in the order given. Pour into a greased loaf pan. Bake at 375° for 50 to 55 minutes. Remove from pan and brush with melted butter.

Yield: 10 servings

The yeast for this dense, biscuitlike bread comes from the beer. The alcohol in the beer cooks away. So easy and so good.

FIVE & UNDER

5 Ingredients or Less

Do not be afraid of simplicity.

X. MARCEL BOULESTIN (1878–1943), chef and food writer

Five-Cup Salad

1 CUP CRUSHED PINEAPPLE, DRAINED

1 CUP MANDARIN ORANGES, DRAINED

1 CUP SHREDDED COCONUT

1 CUP MINI MARSHMALLOWS

1 CUP SOUR CREAM

Combine all ingredients and chill.

Yield: 5 to 7 servings

California Blend Casserole

1 (20 OUNCE) BAG FROZEN CALIFORNIA BLEND VEGETABLES

½ POUND PROCESSED CHEESE, FINELY CUBED

½ CUP BUTTER, MELTED

1 SLEEVE BUTTER-FLAVORED CRACKERS, CRUSHED

Cook vegetables according to package directions; drain. Add cheese, stirring gently until melted. Pour vegetables into a lightly greased 2-quart baking dish. Mix butter and crackers; spread over top of casserole. Bake at 350° for 15 minutes.

Yield: 6 servings

Easy, Cheesy Casserole

1 POUND HAMBURGER

1 BOX MACARONI SHELLS AND CHEESE

1 CAN CONDENSED CREAM OF MUSHROOM SOUP

1½ TO 2 CUPS CHEDDAR CHEESE, SHREDDED

Brown hamburger; drain. Prepare macaroni and cheese according to package directions. Combine hamburger, macaroni and cheese, and soup in a 2-quart casserole. Top with cheese. Bake at 350° for 25 to 30 minutes or until heated through.

Yield: 4 servings

Old-Fashioned Fried Chicken

CHICKEN PIECES, WASHED AND TRIMMED OF EXCESS FAT

FLOUR

SALT AND PEPPER

CANOLA OIL

Coat the chicken in flour mixed with desired amount of salt and pepper. In a large, deep skillet, heat ½-inch layer of canola oil. Brown chicken over medium heat, turning often. Chicken needs to cook approximately 40 minutes or until the meat begins to shrink from the bone and is no longer pink.

Yield: Customizable

You can easily coat chicken by placing it along with the flour and seasoning mixture in a brown lunch bag and shaking it.

Chicken Manicotti

1 JAR THREE-CHEESE SPAGHETTI SAUCE

1½ POUNDS CHICKEN BREAST TENDERS

14 MANICOTTI SHELLS, UNCOOKED

⅓ CUP WATER

2½ CUPS MOZZARELLA CHEESE, SHREDDED

In a 9x13-inch glass baking dish, pour a third of the spaghetti sauce. Place chicken tenders into manicotti noodles, using more than one to fill each shell if needed. Place on top of the spaghetti sauce. Pour water into remaining spaghetti sauce in jar; cover and shake well to mix. Pour spaghetti sauce and water mixture over filled manicotti shells in baking dish, making sure to cover pasta completely. Top with mozzarella cheese. Cover and bake at 350° for 1 hour and 20 minutes or until pasta is tender when pierced with a fork.

Yield: 6 servings

Lord, I'm overwhelmed. Between working a full-time job and caring for my family, I often lose sight of You. Please rejuvenate my soul and help me look to You for strength and comfort when I need it most. Remind me that I can't control everything and that it's okay I'm not perfect. Amen.

Crispy Chicken

1 FRYER CHICKEN, CUT UP

½ CUP BUTTERMILK

½ TEASPOON SEASONED SALT

2 CUPS INSTANT MASHED POTATOES MIX

Remove skin from chicken. In a bowl, combine buttermilk and seasoned salt.

Dip chicken pieces in buttermilk mixture; then roll chicken pieces in instant

potatoes. Place in a baking dish and bake at 375° for approximately 1 hour.

Yield: 4 to 6 servings

Chicken Supreme

1 (2.25 OUNCE) JAR DRIED BEEF

SALT AND PEPPER

8 BONELESS, SKINLESS CHICKEN BREASTS

2 SLICES BACON, CUT INTO FOURTHS

1 (26 OUNCE) CAN CONDENSED CREAM OF CHICKEN OR MUSHROOM SOUP

2 CUPS SOUR CREAM

Cut beef into ½-inch squares and use to line an 11x13-inch pan. Salt and pepper
chicken breasts to taste, and layer on top of the beef. Top each chicken breast
with a portion of bacon. Blend together soup and sour cream; pour over meat.
Cover pan with foil and bake at 250° for 4 hours. Uncover for last 30 minutes.
Serve with mashed potatoes or noodles, using sauce for a savory gravy.

Yield: 8 servings

Chicken Nuggets

2 CUPS SOUR CREAM AND ONION–FLAVORED POTATO CHIPS, CRUSHED

2 TABLESPOONS MILK

6 CHICKEN BREAST FILLETS, CUT INTO 1½-INCH CUBES

⅓ CUP BUTTER, MELTED

1 EGG

Spread the crushed chips in a shallow dish. In a shallow bowl, beat together the egg and milk. Dip chicken cubes in the egg mixture, then dredge them in the chips. Place chicken nuggets on a baking sheet and drizzle them with butter. Bake at 375° for 15 to 18 minutes or until golden brown. Chicken nuggets can be frozen after baking. Serve them with your favorite sauce, such as honey mustard or ranch dressing.

Yield: 6 servings

Chicken Roll-Ups

6 BONELESS, SKINLESS CHICKEN BREASTS

1 CAN SPINACH, DRAINED

1 CUP CHEDDAR CHEESE, SHREDDED

1 CAN CONDENSED CREAM OF CHICKEN SOUP

⅓ CUP MILK

Lightly spray a 9x13-inch baking dish with oil. Use a rolling pin to flatten chicken to approximately ¼ inch. Very large chicken breasts may need to be sliced horizontally. Place chicken in the baking dish. Top with a small handful of spinach and approximately 2 tablespoons of cheese. Roll up each breast, starting with the short end. Hold in place with a toothpick. Blend soup with milk and pour over chicken. Bake at 375° for 1 hour and 10 minutes.

Yield: 6 servings

Smothered Beef Roast

4 POUNDS BEEF ROAST

1 CAN CONDENSED CREAM OF MUSHROOM SOUP

½ CUP BUTTER

2½ TO 3 CUPS WATER

1 LARGE ONION, CHOPPED

Place roast, soup, butter, water, and onion in a large roasting pan. Bake at 325°
for 3 to 4 hours.

Yield: 8 servings

*For me, a great stress reliever is to enjoy my
food someplace other than the kitchen. Get out
there and try dinner with a view of the sunset,
in front of a blazing fire, on the front porch during
a rain shower, or in the woods on a soft picnic blanket.*

BBQ Pork Kabobs

1 POUND BONELESS PORK LOIN, CUT INTO 1½-INCH CHUNKS

8 SMALL WHOLE MUSHROOMS

2 ONIONS, CUT INTO CHUNKS

1 GREEN BELL PEPPER, CUT INTO CHUNKS

⅓ CUP HICKORY-FLAVORED BARBECUE SAUCE

Prepare and heat grill. Thread pork, mushrooms, onion, and green pepper on metal skewers. Place kabobs on the grill and brush with barbecue sauce. Cook 12 to 14 minutes, turning often and brushing with sauce, until pork is thoroughly cooked.

Yield: 4 servings

Key Wonder-Dish Ingredient

10 POUNDS GROUND BEEF

5 MEDIUM ONIONS, CHOPPED

5 MEDIUM GREEN BELL PEPPERS, CHOPPED

5 CLOVES GARLIC, MINCED

1 TEASPOON SALT

Place all ingredients in a very large stockpot and cook over medium heat, stirring frequently until all meat is browned. Drain grease. Cool on a baking sheet lined with paper towels. Divide 1½- to 2-cup portions into plastic freezer bags.

If you take some time one evening to prepare this ingredient, it will make supper for many nights a snap. The meat mixture thaws quickly and will go into a number of staple dishes, such as chili, spaghetti sauce, tacos, burritos, nachos, pizza, sloppy Joes, a casserole, or even vegetable soup. Don't forget to label your bags with the contents and date.

Cheesy Mushroom Burgers

1 TABLESPOON OLIVE OIL

½ CUP FRESH MUSHROOMS, FINELY CHOPPED

1 POUND GROUND BEEF

4 SLICES PROVOLONE CHEESE

4 ENGLISH MUFFINS, SPLIT AND TOASTED

Cook mushrooms in olive oil until tender and brown. Add to ground beef and mix gently. Form into 4 burgers; refrigerate for 1 hour or until firm. Prepare and heat grill. Cook burgers for 10 to 12 minutes, turning once. Top burgers with cheese; cover grill and cook 1 additional minute or until cheese is melted. Serve on English muffins.

Yield: 4 servings

When grilling meat, don't pierce it with a fork or knife. This will let out the juices, and your meat will dry out.

Family-Barbecue Burgers

4 TO 6 HAMBURGER PATTIES

1 CUP KETCHUP

2 TABLESPOONS MUSTARD

½ CUP SUGAR

1 TABLESPOON VINEGAR

Grill hamburgers until done. Combine ketchup, mustard, sugar, and vinegar.

Place spoonfuls of mixture in the bottom of a shallow baking dish; place

grilled hamburger patties on top. Pour remaining sauce over the burgers. Bake,

covered, at 325° for 1 hour.

Yield: 4 to 6 servings

Spaghetti Skillet

1 JAR SPAGHETTI SAUCE WITH MUSHROOMS

1½ CUPS WATER

1 POUND FROZEN MEATBALLS

2 HANDFULS SPAGHETTI NOODLES, BROKEN IN HALF

1 CUP MOZZARELLA CHEESE, SHREDDED

Combine spaghetti sauce and water in a skillet; stir to combine. Bring to a boil. Add meatballs and spaghetti noodles. Stir well, making sure to cover noodles completely. Cover, reduce heat, and simmer for 25 minutes, stirring frequently. Add more water if the mixture appears to be too dry. Cook until spaghetti reaches desired tenderness. Serve topped with cheese.

Yield: 4 servings

"Whatever's in the Kitchen" Skillet

2 TABLESPOONS VEGETABLE OIL

3 TO 4 POTATOES, SLICED

1 POUND GROUND BEEF

1 GREEN BELL PEPPER, CHOPPED

4 EGGS

Cook potatoes in vegetable oil until they reach desired tenderness. In a separate skillet, brown ground beef; drain. Add cooked ground beef and green pepper to potatoes. Beat eggs in a small bowl and pour over potato and ground beef mixture. Cook over medium heat until eggs are done.

Yield: 3 to 4 servings

Five-Ingredient One-Dish Meal

1 POUND GROUND BEEF

1 CAN CUT GREEN BEANS, DRAINED

1 CAN WHOLE-KERNEL CORN, DRAINED

1 CAN CONDENSED CREAM OF MUSHROOM SOUP

4 CUPS MASHED POTATOES, PREPARED

Brown ground beef; drain. In a 2-quart casserole dish, combine beef, beans, corn, and soup. Cover with mashed potatoes. Bake at 375° for 25 to 30 minutes or until browned and heated through.

Yield: 4 servings

Quick 'n' Easy Enchiladas

1 (10 OUNCE) CAN CHICKEN

1 (24 OUNCE) JAR SALSA, DIVIDED

2 CUPS CHEDDAR CHEESE, SHREDDED AND DIVIDED

8 MEDIUM FLOUR TORTILLAS

Drain and shred chicken. Mix with 2 cups salsa and 1 cup cheese. Spoon a quarter of the mixture down the center of each tortilla. Roll up tortillas and place seam side down in a 7x11-inch baking dish. Evenly spread remaining salsa over tortillas, then sprinkle with remaining cheese. Bake at 350° for 30 minutes.

Yield: 8 servings

When you pray, do you often find you're talking to God entirely about yourself? I need... I want... Help me... Remember to ask God to help and bless others. Be courageous...and ask Him to use you to impact the life of someone in need.

Be still before the Lord and wait patiently for him.
PSALM 37:7

Grilled Zucchini Pizza

1 MEDIUM ZUCCHINI

2 CUPS ITALIAN DRESSING

1 CUP PIZZA SAUCE

1½ CUPS MOZZARELLA CHEESE, SHREDDED

Cut zucchini into rounds ½ inch thick. Soak in Italian dressing for 30 minutes. Place on a hot grill. Cook for 3 to 5 minutes, then turn. Top with a spoonful of sauce and a pinch of cheese. Cook until cheese is melted. Remove from grill and serve immediately.

Yield: 4 to 6 servings

Pizza Crescent Bake

2 TUBES REFRIGERATED CRESCENT ROLL DOUGH

1½ POUNDS GROUND BEEF

1 (15 OUNCE) JAR PIZZA SAUCE

2 CUPS MOZZARELLA CHEESE, SHREDDED

Unroll one tube of crescent rolls; place in a lightly greased 9x13-inch baking dish. Press to seal perforations. Set aside. Brown ground beef; drain. Sprinkle beef over dough. Top with pizza sauce and cheese. Unroll remaining tube of crescent rolls; place over cheese layer and press to seal perforations. Bake at 350° for 30 minutes.

Yield: 6 servings

Sausage 'n' Cheese Pinwheels

1 TUBE REFRIGERATED PIZZA DOUGH

½ CUP PIZZA SAUCE

½ POUND ITALIAN SAUSAGE, COOKED AND CRUMBLED

1 CUP MOZZARELLA CHEESE, SHREDDED

1 TABLESPOON SESAME SEEDS

Spread pizza dough onto a rectangular baking sheet. Spread sauce over dough, leaving 3 inches of dough uncovered on each side. Sprinkle sausage and cheese over sauce. Roll up dough, starting with the long end. Seal sides and edges. Brush roll lightly with water and sprinkle with sesame seeds. Bake at 375° for 20 to 25 minutes or until lightly browned. Cut into 8 pinwheels.

Yield: 4 servings

Shepherd's Pie

1 POUND GROUND BEEF

1 SMALL ONION, CHOPPED

2 CUPS FROZEN MIXED VEGETABLES

1 CAN CONDENSED CREAM OF MUSHROOM SOUP

3 CUPS MASHED POTATOES, PREPARED AND REFRIGERATED

In a large skillet, brown ground beef with onion; drain. Stir in vegetables and soup; cook until hot, approximately 5 minutes. Place mixture in a 9-inch pie plate, then spoon mashed potatoes over top. Bake at 375° for 45 minutes or until potatoes are golden brown and pie is bubbling.

Yield: 6 servings

Speedy Beefy Stroganoff

1½ POUNDS GROUND BEEF

1 MEDIUM ONION, CHOPPED

2 CANS CONDENSED CHEDDAR CHEESE SOUP

1 CAN SLICED MUSHROOMS WITH JUICE

SALT AND PEPPER TO TASTE

In a large skillet, brown ground beef with onion; drain. Stir in soup and mushrooms. Season to taste. Simmer until heated through. Serve over noodles, rice, or toast.

Yield: 4 to 6 servings

Simplify your life by posting your grocery list on the refrigerator. Anytime a family member uses up the last of something, they're responsible for adding it to the list.

Cheesy Meatball Meal

1 (18 OUNCE) PACKAGE FROZEN MEATBALLS, THAWED

1 (16 OUNCE) PACKAGE FROZEN VEGETABLE STIR-FRY MIXTURE, THAWED

2 CUPS PLAIN SPAGHETTI SAUCE

1 CUP MOZZARELLA CHEESE, SHREDDED

¼ CUP GRATED PARMESAN CHEESE

Combine meatballs, stir-fry mixture, and spaghetti sauce in a glass baking dish. Top with cheeses. Bake at 350° for 25 minutes or until casserole is bubbling and cheese is melted.

Yield: 6 servings

Bacon-Wrapped Pork Chops

4 BONELESS PORK CHOPS

4 SLICES PEPPER BACON

PEPPER

GARLIC SALT

Wrap each pork chop in one bacon slice. Season with pepper and garlic salt as desired. Place in a shallow buttered baking dish and bake at 350° for 45 minutes or until pork chops are done.

Yield: 4 servings

Super-Quick Meat Loaf

1 POUND GROUND BEEF

1 ENVELOPE DRY ONION SOUP MIX

1 JAR PLAIN SPAGHETTI SAUCE

Mix ground beef and onion soup mix; divide and shape into two loaves. Place loaves in a deep baking dish. Pour spaghetti sauce over loaves. Bake at 350° for 1 hour

Yield: 4 servings

If you're the first person to arrive home in the afternoon, make an effort to greet your family members at the door with a smile! This simple gesture will make them feel loved and appreciated.

Tuna Tortellini

1 POUND FROZEN CHEESE TORTELLINI

2 CUPS FROZEN EARLY PEAS

1 (12 OUNCE) CAN TUNA IN OLIVE OIL (OIL IS ESSENTIAL)

SALT AND PEPPER TO TASTE

GRATED PARMESAN CHEESE

Cook tortellini according to package directions. Add peas to the pot during the last minute of cooking; drain. Return tortellini and peas to the pot and add the tuna in its oil, along with salt and pepper to taste. Heat through, stirring gently. Serve hot with cheese sprinkled on top.

Yield: 4 servings

Kid-Pleasing Soufflé

4 EGGS

2 TABLESPOONS MILK

SALT AND PEPPER TO TASTE

3 TABLESPOONS SHREDDED CHEESE

In a large, microwave-safe bowl, beat eggs; add milk and seasoning. Stir in cheese. Microwave on HIGH for 4 minutes.

Yield: 2 servings

SIMPLY SWEET

Candies & Desserts

In cooking, as in all the arts, simplicity is the sign of perfection.

CURNONSKY (1872–1956), French writer

Quick 'n' Easy Fudge

2 (8 OUNCE) BOXES SEMISWEET CHOCOLATE SQUARES

1 (14 OUNCE) CAN SWEETENED CONDENSED MILK

1 CUP WALNUTS, CHOPPED

2 TEASPOONS VANILLA

Place chocolate and milk in a microwave-safe bowl. Microwave on HIGH until chocolate melts, stirring often. Add walnuts and vanilla; stir. Pour into a buttered 9x9-inch pan. Refrigerate before serving.

Yield: 9 servings

Stuffed 'n' Sugared Dates

1 SMALL BOX WHOLE DATES
WALNUT HALVES, BROKEN IN HALF
SUGAR

Stuff each date with a piece of walnut. Roll the dates in a small bowl of sugar.

Voilá! Your treat is ready.

Yield: 12 servings

Create some time for daily spiritual renewal. Relax in your favorite chair with hot tea, your Bible, a devotional, and a simple treat. Enjoy!

Potato Candy

½ CUP PREPARED MASHED POTATOES
1 POUND POWDERED SUGAR
½ CUP PEANUT BUTTER
FOOD COLORING (OPTIONAL)

In a medium bowl, mix potatoes and sugar. Roll out mixture into a rectangle on a sheet of waxed paper. Spread peanut butter on top. Starting with the short end, roll the candy into a log. Chill and slice thin.

Yield: 8 servings

This old-time recipe is a great way to get rid of left over mashed potatoes.

Anytime Treats

1 PACKAGE GRAHAM CRACKERS
MINI MARSHMALLOWS
SEMISWEET CHOCOLATE CHIPS

Line cookie sheet with graham crackers. Sprinkle crackers with mini marshmallows and chocolate chips. Bake at 350° for 5 minutes or until chocolate chips begin to melt. Cool before serving.

Yield: 4 servings

Easy Graham Browns

2 CUPS GRAHAM CRACKER CRUMBS

1 (14 OUNCE) CAN SWEETENED CONDENSED MILK

1 TEASPOON VANILLA

¾ CUP MINI SEMISWEET CHOCOLATE CHIPS

Blend graham cracker crumbs, milk, and vanilla in a bowl. Stir in chocolate chips. Spread in a lightly greased 9x9-inch pan. Bake at 350° for 20 to 25 minutes. These bars can be frosted if desired.

Yield: 24 small bars

Popcorn Cake

4 QUARTS POPPED CORN

1 POUND GUMDROPS

½ (12 OUNCE) PACKAGE CANDY-COATED CHOCOLATE PIECES

½ POUND SALTED PEANUTS

½ CUP BUTTER

1 POUND MARSHMALLOWS

½ CUP VEGETABLE OIL

Mix popcorn, gumdrops, chocolate pieces, and peanuts in a large bowl. Place butter, marshmallows, and vegetable oil in a saucepan over low heat. Stir until marshmallows are melted. Pour over popcorn mixture and stir. Immediately place in a greased 9x13-inch pan and press firmly. Cool before cutting into squares.

Yield: 16 servings

Read a fun, food-themed storybook with your kids— there are lots to choose from, covering everything from cookies to pancakes. When you've finished reading the story, prepare that particular food with your children. They will always remember this special time you spent with them.

Seven-Layer Bars

½ CUP MARGARINE

1 CUP GRAHAM CRACKER CRUMBS

1 CUP CHOCOLATE CHIPS

1 CUP BUTTERSCOTCH CHIPS

½ TO 1 CUP NUTS, CHOPPED

1 CUP SHREDDED COCONUT

1 (14 OUNCE) CAN SWEETENED CONDENSED MILK

In a 9x13-inch pan, cut butter and melt in a 350° oven to coat bottom. Sprinkle graham cracker crumbs on top. Pat down. Scatter chocolate and butterscotch chips, nuts, and coconut on top. Drizzle milk over top. Bake for 30 minutes or until lightly browned.

Yield: 16 servings

These ingredients are great for layering in a quart jar and giving away as a gift. The last thing that goes in is the graham cracker crumbs, and all the recipient has to add are the butter and the condensed milk.

Dirt Cake

¼ CUP BUTTER, SOFTENED

1 (8 OUNCE) PACKAGE CREAM CHEESE, SOFTENED

1 CUP POWDERED SUGAR

2 SMALL PACKAGES INSTANT VANILLA PUDDING

3½ CUPS MILK

20 OUNCES CHOCOLATE SANDWICH COOKIES, CRUSHED

12 OUNCES WHIPPED TOPPING

Line a 10-inch unused flowerpot with foil. In a bowl, cream butter, cream cheese, and sugar. In a separate bowl, prepare pudding with milk. Combine pudding and cheese mixtures. Fold in whipped topping. In the flowerpot, layer cookie crumbs and pudding several times, ending with crumbs on top. If desired, stick gummy worms and a silk flower on top and serve with a brand-new garden spade.

Yield: 8 servings

Carrot Cake

1¾ CUPS FLOUR

½ TEASPOON BAKING SODA

1 TEASPOON CINNAMON

¼ TEASPOON SALT

1½ CUPS SUGAR

½ TEASPOON NUTMEG

3 EGGS

1 CUP VEGETABLE OIL

1 CUP CARROTS, GRATED

1 CUP PECANS, FINELY CHOPPED

Sift all dry ingredients. Add eggs and oil; mix well. Add carrots and pecans; stir until well mixed. Bake at 350° for 55 minutes. Best topped with a cream cheese frosting.

Yield: 16 servings

When you don't have the time or patience for sifting and just need to blend your dry ingredients, place all dry ingredients in a small bowl and blend with a wire whisk.

Date Roll

1 POUND DATES, CHOPPED

1 POUND NUTS, CHOPPED

1 POUND MINI MARSHMALLOWS

1 POUND GRAHAM CRACKERS, CRUSHED

1 CUP HEAVY WHIPPING CREAM

Combine all ingredients. Roll out mixture into a rectangle on a sheet of waxed paper. Starting with the long end, roll the candy into a log. Wrap in plastic or foil and freeze. Cut into slices and serve.

Yield: 16 servings

Pink Stuff

1 (20 OUNCE) CAN CHERRY PIE FILLING

1 (20 OUNCE) CAN CRUSHED PINEAPPLE, DRAINED

1 (14 OUNCE) CAN SWEETENED CONDENSED MILK

8 OUNCES WHIPPED TOPPING

½ CUP WALNUTS OR PECANS, CHOPPED (OPTIONAL)

Combine all ingredients. Chill. Pink Stuff also can be served frozen.

Yield: 12 to 14 servings

Overwhelmed with the busyness of life? Set aside the "have-tos" and do something just for you—read a book, go for a walk, play with the kids, take a much-needed nap, give yourself a pedicure.... The household chores will wait till tomorrow!

Striped-Cookie Dessert

2 CUPS BUTTERMILK

16 OUNCES WHIPPED TOPPING

2 SMALL PACKAGES INSTANT VANILLA PUDDING

2 SMALL CANS MANDARIN ORANGES, DRAINED

1 PACKAGE FUDGE-STRIPED COOKIES, FROZEN AND CRUSHED

Combine all ingredients except cookies. Refrigerate until ready to serve. Stir in cookies just before serving.

Yield: 10 to 12 servings

You can easily crush candy bars, too, by freezing them first, then placing them in a plastic bag and breaking them with a rolling pin.

Punch Bowl Dessert

2 SMALL PACKAGES INSTANT VANILLA PUDDING

3⅓ CUPS MILK

1 (12 OUNCE) CONTAINER WHIPPED TOPPING, DIVIDED

1 BOX VANILLA WAFERS

1 LARGE CAN CRUSHED PINEAPPLE, DRAINED

3 BANANAS, SLICED

Mix pudding with milk and half of whipped topping. Place one layer of wafers in a clear glass serving bowl; top with half of pineapple, half of bananas, and half of pudding mixture; repeat. Top with remaining whipped topping. Refrigerate until ready to serve.

Yield: 10 to 12 servings

Cinnamon Apple Crisp

6 APPLES, SLICED

1 CUP WATER

1 BOX WHITE CAKE MIX

1 CUP BROWN SUGAR

½ CUP MARGARINE, MELTED

1 TEASPOON CINNAMON

VANILLA ICE CREAM

Arrange apples in the bottom of an ungreased 9x13-inch pan; top with water. In separate bowl combine cake mix, brown sugar, melted margarine, and cinnamon; stir until blended (mixture will be crumbly). Sprinkle crumb mixture over apple slices. Bake at 350° for 50 minutes or until lightly browned and bubbly. Serve warm with vanilla ice cream.

Yield: 16 servings

Use up extra apples with this yummy treat! Cut apples into thin slices and fry them in a greased skillet until tender. Sprinkle with a cinnamon-sugar mixture and enjoy. Especially good with vanilla ice cream!

Fresh Peach Cobbler

BASE:

1 CUP FLOUR

1½ TEASPOONS BAKING POWDER

PINCH SALT

½ CUP BUTTER

½ CUP MILK

TOPPING:

2 CUPS FRESH PEACHES, SLICED

1 CUP HOT WATER

1 CUP SUGAR

PINCH SALT

1 TEASPOON VANILLA

Mix together dry base ingredients. Melt butter and add milk; beat together with dry mixture and pour into a lightly buttered 7x11-inch baking dish. Combine topping ingredients and pour over batter. Bake at 350° for 1 hour.

Yield: 8 to 10 servings

Under-ripe peaches, pears, or nectarines can foil your recipe plans. Try slicing the fruit and placing it in a saucepan with apple or orange juice. Add a bit of cinnamon and simmer the fruit in juice for 5 minutes. Chill and add to your recipe.

Quick 'n' Easy Cherry Cobbler

2 (20 OUNCE) CANS CHERRY PIE FILLING

1 BOX YELLOW CAKE MIX

1¼ STICKS MARGARINE, MELTED

1 CUP WALNUTS

Pour both cans of pie filling into a 9x13-inch baking dish. Spread dry cake mix over filling. Top with melted margarine and walnuts. Bake at 350° for 35 to 45 minutes. Serve warm with vanilla ice cream.

Yield: 16 servings

Mix this cobbler recipe up a bit.
Try apple pie filling instead of cherry.
And instead of walnuts, use pecans. Yum!

Wacky Cake

3 CUPS FLOUR

2 CUPS SUGAR

½ CUP COCOA

2 TEASPOONS BAKING SODA

1 TEASPOON SALT

⅔ CUP OIL

2 TEASPOONS VANILLA

2 TABLESPOONS VINEGAR

2 CUPS WARM WATER

Sift flour, sugar, cocoa, baking soda, and salt into a large mixing bowl. Make three wells in the dry mix. Pour the oil and vanilla in one well, the vinegar in another, and the water in the third. Mix well. Pour into a greased 9x13-inch pan that has been dusted with cocoa. Bake at 350° for 35 minutes.

Yield: 16 servings

When you take a cake from the oven, place it on a watersoaked towel for a very short time. The cooled cake will turn out of the pan without sticking.

Roman Apple Cake

4 CUPS APPLES, CHOPPED

2 CUPS SUGAR

½ CUP OIL

2 TEASPOONS VANILLA

2 EGGS

2 CUPS FLOUR

2 TEASPOONS CINNAMON

2 TEASPOONS BAKING SODA

1 TEASPOON SALT

1 CUP NUTS, CHOPPED

Blend all ingredients until well moistened. Place in a 9x13-inch pan and bake at 350° for 40 minutes.

Yield: 16 servings

Reuse a large spice container with the removable shaker shield. Fill the container with flour and label it clearly. Use the flour to dust your greased baking pans.

Chocolate Chip Cheesecake

3 (8 OUNCE) PACKAGES CREAM CHEESE

3 EGGS

¾ CUP SUGAR

1 TEASPOON VANILLA

3 TUBES REFRIGERATED CHOCOLATE CHIP COOKIE DOUGH

Beat together cream cheese, eggs, sugar, and vanilla; set aside. Slice cookie dough into ⅓-inch slices. Arrange half of the cookie dough slices on the bottom of a greased 9x13-inch glass baking dish. Press slices together so no holes remain. Spoon cream cheese mixture evenly over top. Cover with remaining cookie dough. Bake at 350° for 45 to 50 minutes. Remove from oven and allow to cool. Refrigerate. Do not cut until well chilled.

Yield: 16 servings

Make your own pan coating: mix equal parts shortening, vegetable oil, and flour. Mix thoroughly and store, covered, in the refrigerator. Use this mixture at room temperature to coat baking pans instead of using a spray or other method. It works wonders!

If I make anything homemade, it'll be dessert... definitely not pan coating!

The Ultimate Chocolate Chip Bar

1 CUP BUTTER, MELTED

1 CUP BROWN SUGAR

1 CUP SUGAR

2 EGGS

1 TEASPOON VANILLA

2 CUPS FLOUR

½ TEASPOON SALT

1 TEASPOON SODA

½ TEASPOON BAKING POWDER

2 CUPS QUICK ROLLED OATS

1 (24 OUNCE) PACKAGE SEMISWEET CHOCOLATE CHIPS

Grease a 9x13-inch pan. Mix ingredients in the order given and spread in pan.

Bake at 350° for 20 to 25 minutes. Cool and cut into squares.

Yield: 16 servings

Gather your family together once a week for devotions and dessert. Read through a family-friendly devotional book or study a passage from the Bible. End with prayer and a sweet treat!

Rejoice in the Lord always. I will say it again: Rejoice!

PHILIPPIANS 4:4

Cinnamon-Cream Cheese Squares

(You can't eat just one!)

2 TUBES REFRIGERATED CRESCENT ROLL DOUGH

1 CUP SUGAR

2 (8 OUNCE) PACKAGES CREAM CHEESE, SOFTENED

¼ CUP BUTTER, MELTED

¼ CUP SUGAR MIXED WITH 2 TEASPOONS CINNAMON

Roll out one tube of crescent roll dough to cover the bottom of a lightly greased 9x13-inch pan. Combine 1 cup sugar and cream cheese and spread over dough. Pat remaining dough over top. Brush melted butter on top of the dough; sprinkle with cinnamon sugar. Bake at 375° for 25 minutes. Cut into squares. Yield: 16 servings

Make greasing a pan with shortening mess-free by placing a plastic sandwich bag over your hand to spread the shortening onto the pan. When done, just throw the bag away.

Sunflower Cookies

¾ **CUP WHOLE-WHEAT FLOUR**

½ **CUP WHEAT GERM**

2 **TABLESPOONS DRY BUTTERMILK POWDER**

½ **TEASPOON BAKING SODA**

¼ **CUP BUTTER (NO SUBSTITUTES), SOFTENED**

¼ **CUP APPLESAUCE**

½ **CUP BROWN SUGAR**

1 **EGG**

½ **TEASPOON VANILLA**

1 **CUP RAISINS (OR MINI SEMI-SWEET CHOCOLATE CHIPS)**

½ **CUP SUNFLOWER SEEDS**

½ **CUP WALNUTS, CHOPPED**

Combine flour, wheat germ, buttermilk powder, and baking soda; set aside. Blend butter, applesauce, and sugar until fluffy; add egg and vanilla, blending well. Add flour mixture to butter mixture until well combined. Stir in raisins (or chocolate chips), sunflower seeds, and nuts. Drop by rounded teaspoons onto a greased baking sheet (or an ungreased baking stone). Bake at 350° for 8 to 12 minutes.

Yield: 3 dozen

Give the stresses of your day to God. He wants you to!

Praise be to the Lord, to God our Savior, who daily bears our burdens.
PSALM 68:19

Blue Tomato Bars

4 CUPS GREEN TOMATO, FINELY CHOPPED

2 CUPS BROWN SUGAR, DIVIDED

¾ CUPS BUTTER, SOFTENED

1½ CUPS FLOUR

1 TEASPOON BAKING SODA

1 TEASPOON SALT

2 CUPS OATMEAL

½ CUP NUTS, CHOPPED

1 CUP BLUEBERRIES (FRESH OR FROZEN)

In a saucepan, cook tomato and 1 cup brown sugar over low heat. In a mixing bowl, cream butter and remaining 1 cup brown sugar; add flour, baking soda, salt, oatmeal, and nuts. Grease a 9x13-inch pan. Measure out 2½ cups dough and press into bottom of pan. Spread tomato mixture, including juice, on top. Sprinkle berries over tomatoes. Crumble the remaining dough and sprinkle over all. Bake at 375° for 30 to 35 minutes.

Yield: 16 servings

Zucchini Brownies

2 CUPS FLOUR

½ CUP COCOA

1½ TEASPOONS BAKING SODA

1 TEASPOON SALT

2 CUPS GRATED ZUCCHINI

½ CUP VEGETABLE OIL

½ CUP WATER

2 TEASPOONS VANILLA

1¼ CUPS SUGAR

½ CUP NUTS, CHOPPED (OPTIONAL)

Blend flour, cocoa, baking soda, and salt; set aside. In a large bowl, combine zucchini, vegetable oil, water, and vanilla. Stir in sugar, then add dry mix. Stir in nuts if desired, then spread in a greased 9x13-inch pan. Bake at 350° for 25 to 30 minutes. Top cooled brownies with a chocolate frosting of your choice. Yield: 16 servings

I've found a sneaky way to get kids—and adults—to eat their veggies. Blue Tomato Bars are a fun way to use up the garden's unripened tomatoes. The blueberries hide the telltale veggie green. Zucchini Brownies are the best, moistest cake brownies I've ever tasted. Enjoy these creative additions to your supper menu.

Sulinda's Toffee Brownies

½ CUP MARGARINE, SOFTENED

½ CUP BROWN SUGAR

½ CUP SUGAR

1 TEASPOON VANILLA

2 EGGS

1½ CUPS FLOUR

1 TEASPOON BAKING POWDER

DASH SALT

1 (10 OUNCE) BAG TOFFEE BITS

Cream margarine, sugars, vanilla, and eggs. Add dry ingredients. Spread in a greased 9x13-inch pan. Bake at 350° for 30 minutes.

Yield: 16 servings

Crunch Brownies

1¼ CUPS MILK CHOCOLATE CHIPS, DIVIDED

⅓ CUP BUTTER, SOFTENED

¾ CUP SUGAR

2 EGGS, BEATEN

1 TEASPOON VANILLA

1 CUP FLOUR

½ TEASPOON BAKING POWDER

¼ TEASPOON SALT

⅓ CUP CRISP RICE CEREAL

Place ½ cup chocolate chips in a small microwave-safe bowl. Microwave on HIGH for 15 seconds; stir. Repeat at 15-second intervals until melted. In a medium bowl, cream butter and sugar. Blend in beaten eggs, then add melted chocolate and vanilla. Combine flour, baking powder, and salt; add to chocolate mixture, stirring well. Spread into a lightly greased 9x9-inch inch pan. Bake at 350° for 25 minutes. Sprinkle with remaining chocolate chips and bake 2 minutes longer. Spread chocolate over top and sprinkle cereal by hand, pressing in lightly.

Yield: 24 bars

If your cupboards are organized like mine, your baking products are all in the same general area. That means you probably have your baking soda stored near spices or other items that give off an odor the baking soda could naturally absorb. As soon as you bring baking soda home from the store, place it in an airtight container. Even unopened, over time the cardboard box can allow the baking soda to become tainted.

Low-Sugar, Low-Fat Strawberry Pie

2 CUPS COLD WATER

1 PACKAGE SUGAR-FREE VANILLA COOK PUDDING

1 PACKAGE SUGAR-FREE STRAWBERRY GELATIN

4 CUPS STRAWBERRIES, SLICED

1 (9 INCH) GRAHAM CRACKER CRUST

1 (8 OUNCE) CONTAINER LIGHT WHIPPED TOPPING

In a saucepan, mix pudding into water. Bring to a boil, stirring constantly. Add gelatin, stirring until dissolved. Remove from heat and cool for 10 minutes. Add strawberries, then pour into crust. Refrigerate until set. Top with whipped topping.

Yield: 8 servings

Low-Fat Pistachio-Nut Cake

CAKE:

1 BOX YELLOW CAKE MIX

1 BOX SUGAR-FREE PISTACHIO PUDDING

1 CUP FAT-FREE SOUR CREAM

½ CUP APPLESAUCE

4 EGGS

½ TEASPOON ALMOND EXTRACT

FILLING:

½ CUP WALNUTS, CHOPPED

¼ CUP SUGAR

1 TEASPOON CINNAMON

Combine cake ingredients; pour half of the batter into a greased Bundt pan. Combine filling ingredients; sprinkle half over the batter in the pan. Add remaining batter and top with remaining nut mixture. Bake at 350° for 55 minutes.

Yield: 12 to 14 servings

Most days I enjoy my desserts in moderation and care little about their fat and sugar content, but these two new pie and cake recipes make "diet" foods fun and oh so tasty.

Cheesecake in a Snap

1 (8 OUNCE) PACKAGE CREAM CHEESE, SOFTENED

1 (14 OUNCE) CAN SWEETENED CONDENSED MILK

1 (9 INCH) GRAHAM CRACKER CRUST

1 (20 OUNCE) CAN CHERRY PIE FILLING

In a medium bowl, beat cream cheese until smooth and fluffy. Add milk and mix until well blended. Pour into crust and chill. Top with pie filling.

Yield: 8 servings

Nifty Substitutions

A Little of This, Plus a Pinch of That

Have you ever started to mix together ingredients for a recipe, only to find that you're missing an important item? Don't fret! Before you toss what you're preparing—and before running all the way to the grocery store—check out this list. We've found that the following substitutes work wonders when you're in a pinch.

ALLSPICE

1 teaspoon allspice = ½ teaspoon cinnamon plus ½ teaspoon ground cloves

BAKING POWDER

1 teaspoon baking powder = ¼ teaspoon baking soda plus ⅝ teaspoon cream of tartar

BUTTERMILK

1 cup buttermilk = 1 cup milk plus 1 tablespoon lemon juice or white vinegar (let stand 5 minutes before using)

BROWN SUGAR

½ cup brown sugar (firmly packed) = 1 cup white sugar or ½ cup white sugar plus 2 tablespoons molasses

CORNSTARCH (FOR THICKENING)

1 tablespoon cornstarch = 2 tablespoons all-purpose flour or 2 tablespoons granular tapioca

CORN SYRUP

1 cup corn syrup = 1 cup sugar plus ¼ cup liquid or 1 cup honey (use whatever liquid is called for in recipe)

GARLIC

1 small clove of fresh garlic = ⅛ teaspoon garlic powder

HERBS

1 tablespoon fresh-cut herbs = 1 teaspoon dried herbs

HONEY

1 cup honey = 1¼ cups sugar and ¼ cup liquid (use whatever liquid is called for in recipe)

LEMON JUICE

1 teaspoon lemon juice = ½ teaspoon vinegar

MUSTARD

1 teaspoon dry mustard = 1 tablespoon prepared mustard

ONION

1 medium onion = 1 tablespoon onion powder

1 small onion = 1 tablespoon dried minced onion

SELF-RISING FLOUR

1 cup sifted self-rising flour = 1 cup sifted all-purpose flour plus
1½ teaspoons baking powder and ½ teaspoon salt

SOUR CREAM

1 cup sour cream = 1 cup plain yogurt or 1 cup cottage cheese pureed in a
blender with 1 tablespoon lemon juice and ⅓ cup butter

UNSWEETENED BAKING CHOCOLATE

1 ounce unsweetened baking chocolate = 3 tablespoons unsweetened cocoa
plus 1 tablespoon butter or shortening

VANILLA BEAN

½ bean = 1 tablespoon vanilla extract

WHIPPING CREAM

1 cup whipping cream, unwhipped = 2 cups whipped topping

WINE

1 cup wine = 1 cup grape, cranberry, apple juice, or even chicken broth

Weights and Measures Know-How

The Cheat Sheet

While Martha knows how to convert every kitchen measurement known to womankind, I find that I'm frequently in need of a little help. Please use this cheat sheet when you find you've forgotten how to convert tablespoons to teaspoons, pints to ounces, quarts to cups, and everything in between.

½ tablespoon = 1½ teaspoons

1 tablespoon = 3 teaspoons

¼ cup = 4 tablespoons

⅓ cup = 5 tablespoons + 1 teaspoon

½ cup = 8 tablespoons

½ pint = 1 cup (or 8 fluid ounces)

1 pint = 2 cups (or 16 fluid ounces)

1 quart = 4 cups (or 2 pints or 32 fluid ounces)

1 gallon = 16 cups (or 4 quarts)

1 pound = 16 ounces

1 peck = 8 quarts

1 bushel = 4 pecks

SIMPLY QUICK SNACKS

Almond Crunch Mix 15

Apple Dip 20

Candy Corn Snack Mix... 14

Cheesy Cracker Snack... 26

Cracker Sandwiches... 29

Cucumber Spread.. 22

Dill Pickle Fryers.. 28

Frozen Bananas 19

Frozen Fruit Snack 17

Gooey Banana Crackers.. 19

"It's So Easy!" Veggie Dip.. 26

Munch Mix.. 10

Nachos 'n' Cheese with Salsa 27

Quick Cheesy Fries..27

Quick Club Quesadillas 30

Simple Salsa...24

Spinach Dip..21

Strawberry Graham Snack 18

Sweet Fruit Dip...20

Sweet Snack Mix...11

Taco Dip 23

Traditional Snack Mix 13

Trail Mix 14

Ultimate Snack Mix..12

Veggie Dip 25

Yummy Peanut Butter Balls...16

Meals on the Go

Amish Peanut Butter Spread 32

Anytime Egg Fajitas 46

Apple–Peanut Butter Bagel Sandwiches 39

Baked Pizza Sandwich 38

Best Turkey Bagel 40

Burrito Wraps..42

Cheesy Chicken Potatoes 50

Classic Egg Salad 35

Corned Beef Sandwich 48

Egg Salad with a Twist Sandwich Spread.................................36

Family-Size Gyro..49

Fried Bologna Sandwich 41

Ham 'n' Cheese Rolls 44

Mexican Sandwich Rolls..47

Mini Pizza Delights 37

Pigs in a Blanket 42

Salsa-Potato Burritos 43

Toasty Ham Salad Sandwiches 40

Tuna Cheese Spread..33

Vineyard Chicken Salad..34

Yummy Grilled Cheese 45

Casseroles & Other One-Dish Wonders

45-Minute Casserole..60

BBQ Hamburger Muffins 76

Beefy Noodle Casserole..61

Cheesy Baked Spaghetti...82

Cheesy Chicken Bake 71

Cheesy Noodle Casserole..58

Chicken 'n' Corn Bread Casserole 54

Chicken 'n' Pasta Skillet..81

Chicken 'n' Wild Rice Casserole...55

Chicken Waikiki 67

Chickenetti 87

Country Breakfast Casserole...52

Country-Style Scalloped Potatoes 'n' Ham 88

Creamy Ham 'n' Broccoli Bake 86

Crisp Rice Casserole 57

Curried Honey Chicken 66

Easy Beef Skillet 75

Fiesta Casserole 63

Grandma Shutt's Meat Loaf 69

Ham 'n' Potato Casserole 62

Hamburger Gravy 74

Hash 70

Hawaiian Burgers 73

Home-Style Macaroni 'n' Cheese 80

Home-Style Sausage, Cabbage, and Potatoes 68

Lolita's Summer Zucchini Casserole 59

Macaroni-Sausage Bake 84

Mexican Stuffed Shells 83

No-Peek Steak 78

One-Dish Lasagna 85

Pepper Steak 79

Sausage 'n' Cheese Grits Casserole 53

Super-Easy Chicken Pot Pie 65

Taco Bake 72

Taco Plate 64

Tasty Baked Steak 77

Tuna Noodle Casserole 56

SLOW-COOKER RECIPES

Bacon Chicken 106

BBQ Stew 92

Beef Barley Vegetable Soup 94

Best Barbecue Bites 99

Cheesy Egg 'n' Mushroom Meal 110

Chicken Fajitas 111

Cowboy Stew 93

Creamy Mushroom Pork Chops 107

Crock-Pot Western Omelet 113

Delicious Slow-Cooked Beef Sandwiches 98

Easy Country-Style BBQ Ribs 101

Easy Veggie Soup 96

Hot Italian Sausage Sandwiches 100

Ida's Hobo Stew 91

Pork Ribs 'n' Kraut 102

Pot Roast with Carrots 103

Slow 'n' Easy Spaghetti 108

Slow 'n' Savory Fish Chowder 97

Slow-Cooker Burritos 104

Slow-Cooker Mac 'n' Cheese 109

Sour Cream 'n' Bean Chicken 105

Spicy Beef Stew 90

Split Pea Soup 95

Turkey Rueben Pot 112

Salads, Soups & Sides

Alfredo Pasta Salad 120

Baked Sweet Potatoes 130

Beefy Pasta 'n' Salsa Soup 142

Beer Bread 151

Broccoli 'n' Rice 137

Broccoli Noodle Soup 146

Cheeseburger Chowder 149

Chili 147

Clam Chowder 143

Classic Green Bean Bake 128

Corn Casserole 126

Cream of Broccoli Soup 144

Creamy Noodles 139

Cucumbers with Cream Dressing 116

Fresh Green Beans 129

Grated Potato Salad 123

Grilled Hobo Potatoes 134

Harvard Beets 127

Hawaiian Fruit Salad 125

Heavenly Broccoli Salad 121

Homemade Applesauce 135

Layered Lettuce Salad 119

Make-Ahead Mashed Potato Casserole 132

Mexican Chicken Soup 140

Old-Fashioned Potato Soup 145

Pasta Salad... 136

Pull-Apart Garlic Bread 150

Roasted Ranch Potato Salad 124

Roasted Veggie Medley 133

Spaghetti Slaw 117

Spanish Rice (Wanda's Style) 138

Sweet Potato Casserole 131

Taco Salad..122

Vegetable Soup 141

Waldorf Salad 118

Wheat Chili 148

5 Ingredients or Less

Bacon-Wrapped Pork Chops.. 176

BBQ Pork Kabobs 163

California Blend Casserole.. 154

Cheesy Meatball Meal 176

Cheesy Mushroom Burgers 165

Chicken Manicotti... 157

Chicken Nuggets... 160

Chicken Roll-Ups 161

Chicken Supreme 159

Crispy Chicken 158

Easy, Cheesy Casserole... 155

Family-Barbecue Burgers 166

Five-Cup Salad 154

Five-Ingredient One-Dish Meal 169

Grilled Zucchini Pizza 171

Key Wonder-Dish Ingredient 164

Kid-Pleasing Soufflé 178

Old-Fashioned Fried Chicken 156

Pizza Crescent Bake 172

Quick 'n' Easy Enchiladas 170

Sausage 'n' Cheese Pinwheels 173

Shepherd's Pie 174

Smothered Beef Roast 162

Spaghetti Skillet 167

Speedy Beefy Stroganoff 175

Super-Quick Meat Loaf 177

Tuna Tortellini 178

"Whatever's in the Kitchen" Skillet 168

Candies & Desserts

Anytime Treats 183

Blue Tomato Bars 202

Carrot Cake 188

Cheesecake in a Snap 208

Chocolate Chip Cheesecake 198

Cinnamon Apple Crisp 193

Cinnamon–Cream Cheese Squares 200

Crunch Brownies 205

Date Roll 189

Dirt Cake 187

Easy Graham Browns 184

Fresh Peach Cobbler 194

Low-Fat Pistachio-Nut Cake 207

Low-Sugar, Low-Fat Strawberry Pie 206

Pink Stuff 190

Popcorn Cake 185

Potato Candy 182

Punch Bowl Dessert 192

Quick 'n' Easy Cherry Cobbler 195

Quick 'n' Easy Fudge 180

Roman Apple Cake 197

Seven-Layer Bars 186

Striped-Cookie Dessert 191

Stuffed 'n' Sugared Dates 181

Sulinda's Toffee Brownies 204

Sunflower Cookies 201

Ultimate Chocolate Chip Bar, The 199

Wacky Cake 196

Zucchini Brownies 203

Also Available from Mary & Martha. . .

In the Kitchen with Mary & Martha is not your ordinary cookbook. With two lovable characters, oodles of kitchen tips and heartfelt inspiration, and an overabundance of recipes for delicious dishes (all of which have received the Mary & Martha Stamp of Approval)— this delightful volume is the first in a must-have series for cooks of all ages. The hardback, comb-bound cookbook includes recipes for family favorites—like those gooey cookies Grandma used to make!— and includes adorable illustrations and two-color ink throughout. A guaranteed-to-please package makes this a great gift.

A Cookbook Featuring Oodles of Inspiration, Recipes & Tips

ISBN 1-59310-878-8 / $14.95 U.S.

Coming September 2006

Cookin' Up Christmas with Mary & Martha

Available Wherever Books Are Sold